THE MISSING PEACE

**ESTHER GENDELMAN
AND RACHEL STEIN**

MENUCHA PUBLISHERS

Menucha Publishers, Inc.
© 2016 by Esther Gendelman and Rachel Stein
Typeset and designed by Rivkah Lewis
All rights reserved

ISBN 978-1-61465-411-7

No part of this publication may be translated, reproduced, stored in a retrieval system, or transmitted in any form or by any means, electronic, mechanical, photocopying, recording, or otherwise, without prior permission in writing from both the copyright holder and the publisher.

Published and distributed by:
Menucha Publishers, Inc.
1235 38th Street
Brooklyn, NY 11218
Tel/Fax: 718-232-0856
www.menuchapublishers.com
sales@menuchapublishers.com

Printed in Israel

DAVID PELCOVITZ, PH.D
PSYCHOLOGIST
66 HAMPSHIRE ROAD
GREAT NECK, NY 11023

GENDELMAN AND STEIN HAVE WRITTEN a practical book that provides clear guidelines on how to use self-examination and openness to the perspective of others to deepen and enhance our relationships with family member, friends, and colleagues. Scenarios depicting conflicts between family members and friends or acquaintances allow the reader to manage interpersonal conflict in a manner that can lead to a greater sense of harmony and peace in connection with others. I recommend this book for all who are looking to develop their ability to deepen their relationships in an honest, mature, and meaningful way.

David Pelcovitz

THE CONCEPT FOR THE BOOK IS BRILLIANT. It is truly creative and promises to be very effective.

Rabbi Leib Kelemen

I WOULD LIKE TO CONGRATULATE the authors on their project, which is unlike anything else that has been done before. I wish them tremendous *hatzlachah* in their *avodas hakodesh*!

Rabbi Nachman Seltzer

Dedication

WE DEDICATE THIS BOOK
IN LOVING MEMORY OF OUR DEAR PARENTS,

AVROHOM BEN MOSHE
AND YEHUDIS BAS YERUCHAM,

BOTH OF WHOM PASSED AWAY
IN THE PRIME OF THEIR LIVES.

After our father died, our mother continued to speak about our father lovingly. Despite her shattered dreams of growing old with her husband, she cherished the loving relationship that they had shared over nine years.

The special closeness they shared taught us volumes about the importance of secure, nurturing relationships. We hope we can give them *nachas* as their little girls collaborate on a volume that teaches how to develop and maintain healthy, loving connections.

CONTENTS

Acknowledgments 13
Introduction 17

PART I: All in the Family

I Am Floored! 21
No Pizza For Me?! 27
Can It Be? 33
Mathematically Speaking! 38
Hakol Beseder 42
Hurried and Harried 47
What's the Big Deal? 51

Forlorn and Forgotten ... 56
Porcupine Quills ... 61
Koalas — Here We Come ... 67
Meet Your New Grandson ... 73
Surprise Package ... 79
Tentacles of Fear ... 86
Yikes! Mom's Moving In! ... 91
Shattered Dreams ... 96
Oh Look! ... 102

PART II: *Allies and Alibis*

Fired! ... 111
A Little 'Cell'f Reflection ... 117
Passing the Buck ... 124
"Purr"fectly Understandable ... 132
And the Winner Is... ... 137
A Telling Moment ... 142
Purim Delights ... 149
Triangular Trauma ... 155
Those are the Brakes ... 160
The Extra Mile ... 166
On Call ... 172
Ruling My Roost ... 178
It's a Matter of "Principal" ... 185
Reading between the Lines ... 191

A Work of Art 199
A Piece of the Pie.. 207

PART III: Reclaiming Our Missing Peace

Assessment...217
What's the Big Deal?... 220
Porcupine Quills..227
Fired! 231
Passing the Buck 236
A Telling Moment 241

Conclusion...244

ACKNOWLEDGMENTS

We would like to thank Rabbi Leib Kelemen, Rabbi Dr. David Pelcovitz, and Rabbi Nachman Seltzer for their enthusiastic approbations of our project. You took time from your already demanding schedules of *avodas hakodesh* to give us encouragement, constructive feedback, and *berachos*. We would like to gratefully acknowledge the superior staff of Menucha Publishers. Mrs. Esther Heller's skill and expertise shine through every page, along with her warmth and positivity. It's been a pleasure and a privilege to work with you! To Mr. Hirsch Traube, Mrs. Chaya Baila Lieber, Mrs. Cindy Scarr, Mrs. Rivkah Lewis, and Mrs. Daliya Shapiro — your tireless efforts in transforming our manuscript into a beautiful book are deeply appreciated. From graphics to proofreading, you've done a superlative job. And to our personal editor and proofreader, Gabi, who gave us confidence that this was a worthy manuscript to submit and provided valuable editorial corrections and feedback.

Esther's acknowledgments:

HOW CAN I BEGIN TO acknowledge the many people who shaped my life, influenced me, and guided me at every stage of life? Every encounter offers a learning opportunity. Teachers, students, friends, mentors, colleagues, *shidduch* couples, clients, neighbors, acquaintances, and even critics all taught me valuable knowledge, enhanced my self-awareness, and contributed to my growth. The only possibility is to pay it forward, which is one of my goals with this book.

I want to give a special thank you to my dear in-laws, Mr. and Mrs. I. Gendelman, who provide a sterling example of love and commitment for their children. I am one of your fortunate beneficiaries. Even though we live far away, we feel your warmth in close proximity. May Hashem *bentsh* you with many healthy and happy years together and *nachas* from your children, grandchildren, and great-grandchildren.

I want to thank my very dear friend Dr. Sharon Livingston, who has become a beloved part of our family. To know you is to love you. You radiate sunshine and taught me how to create a space for play no matter how demanding our schedules might be. You transformed my morning cup of coffee into a cherished routine. Thank you for reading every story, providing valuable feedback, and for sharing your expertise as we coauthored the ICARE section of this book together.

Rachel, my one and only sister…we did it together! Yes, I thought I was the "bossy older sister," but who was the taskmaster propelling us forward from the inception of this project until the very last word? I admire your sensitivity, love of giving, patience, and your wonderful contagious laugh that makes our husbands just look at us helplessly until we wipe away the tears and sigh with deep delight. We have shared *simchah* and pain and only become closer through the years. Thank you for the gift of my precious nieces and nephews whom I adore. Thank you for always being there as a loving sister and your willingness to share anything and everything from the *sheitel* on your head to the shoes on your feet. May we always be there for one another and give *nachas* to the memories of our dear parents.

My dearest children, Avrohom Tzvi and Malki, Shimon Ariel and Brochi, Azi and Shaindi, Nachi and Sora, and Sruli — each of you gives us more *nachas* than you can ever realize. Your enthusiastic *avodas Hashem*, your close connection to one another, your continuous striving for growth in *middos*... Raising you from infancy and knowing that our bond only gets deeper fills me with indescribable joy. You truly give hope and inspiration to other parents who came home from teachers' meetings in elementary school needing Tylenol. And watching you as couples building a life together and raising your precious *kinderlach* with love and care gives us endless *simchah* and a few laughs when we see your children behaving in ways that bring back memories. Sruli, thank you for learning in Detroit throughout high school so that we can enjoy watching you *shteig* and cherish our weekly Shabbos meals that you enhance in every way. Although we try to take care of your needs, I believe the reverse is more accurate. Yet, even when you are ready to fly from the nest, we know that you, together with your siblings, will always have a place in our hearts and in our home.

And, Baruch, how do I begin to thank you for over thirty years of marriage? Your love of Torah, devotion to our family, quiet humility, and *ayin tovah* create an environment where I feel loved and cherished, appreciated and encouraged. You patiently waited for your eighteen-year-old *kallah* to grow up and perhaps might still be waiting. There are no words to thank you for being my caring husband and for modeling the gold standard of acceptance and love for our children to emulate.

And finally, I thank Hashem for giving me life and the myriad *berachos* that accompany me every step of the journey.

May Hashem continue to *bentsh* us with His *chesed* and *kol tuv*.

Rachel's acknowledgments:

TO MY HUSBAND, RABBI REUVEN STEIN, for being a constant source of support and encouragement. May we continue to have *nachas* together *ad me'ah v'esrim*.

To Shmuel Yaakov and Chavie, Avrami, Yitzchok and Shiri, Yaakov and Estie, Nesanel and Leah Ettie, Chaim and Bassy, Yehudis Rena and Yehuda, Ahuva, Moshe, Yossi, Rivky, and Tehila — you're the best and I love every one of you. To Mrs. Rita Stein, my devoted and amazing mother-in-law, with love, and to my beloved father-in-law, Mr. Harry Stein, *a"h*, for his unconditional love and making me feel like a daughter.

To my dear sister, Esther — how do two sisters become even closer? By writing a book together! It is my privilege to dedicate this book to the best sister I ever had, an eloquent and astute co-author and a beloved confidante and friend. Your vast accomplishments continue to amaze and inspire me. May Hashem give you continued strength and health *ad me'ah v'esrim* to keep radiating your special light and transforming lives wherever you go.

And last but not least, Esther and I wish to thank Aunt Betty — an outstanding aunt whom we love with full hearts. Thank you for being in our lives; you mean so much to us.

With all my love,
Rachel

INTRODUCTION

How would you feel if you found a treasure chest of gold and jewels? And how would you feel if you found that treasure chest of gold and jewels while stranded alone on a deserted island? How long would the initial blast of happiness last if you had no one to share the discovery with? Healthy relationships with others are among the most special gifts Hashem offers us in This World. Yet, as with any other worthwhile attainment, healthy relationships require sustained effort.

Do you long for supportive, empowering relationships that encourage you to become your ideal self? Throughout our lives, beginning in infancy, we need a smile and the feeling that we matter to someone. Even when our physical needs are met, if we lack emotional validation, it's as if we shrivel up and die inside.

In the absence of loving companionship, there is a sense of loneliness, no matter what else we achieve in life.

The purpose of this book is to provide a glimpse at common relationship pitfalls, which are often difficult to see when our own hurt prevents us from examining ourselves objectively. When reading about others, however, it is as if the pieces of a puzzle join together to form a wonderfully clear picture, beautiful in its wholeness. Once we take the initial steps of self-exploration, we embark on a lifelong journey of enhanced *bein adam l'chaveiro*.

The Missing Peace brings genuine stories of relationship conflicts — between family members, acquaintances, close friends, and everything in between. The unique angle this book provides is that the stories are told from both sides, affording us the unique vantage point of the protagonist and antagonist, offering a fresh, insightful, and previously unexplored perspective. Readers will recognize themselves as they identify with the opposing, yet valid, emotions of both personalities.

Rav Shlomo Wolbe, *ztz"l,* stresses that self-knowledge is the single most important key to growth. It is our hope that this book will provide encouragement and tools for joining the missing pieces (not to mention the missing peace) that are all too often parts of relationships, in addition to guiding your journey toward self-discovery and growth.

PART I

1

I AM FLOORED!

Mommy Speaks:

The call from my married daughter started off innocently enough, but why did I have this sneaking suspicion that she had a deeper agenda than just calling to say hi?

"Hi, Michal, how are you, sweetie?"

She answered with platitudes, and then proceeded to regale me with the latest episodes of the kids' various stages of development. I listened with feigned patience, subduing my yawns and longing to sink into my novel for a few luxurious minutes before falling into bed. But motherhood is based upon love and devotion certainly not offered only when it's convenient.

"So, Meir was diagnosed with a speech and language processing disorder," Michal continued, and suddenly my fatigue vanished as I listened intently, clutching the phone and feeling my daughter's pain. "And the therapist said that's why he has social issues."

"Oh, Michal," I breathed, "I'm sorry."

Thinking of the years of struggle we went through with our Yitzy — he, too, had learning issues and social difficulties — I wondered if Michal blamed our genes for the problems Meir was having. It's not our fault, though, is it? These things are *bashert*, even if genetics are involved. *You know that, right, Michal?*

"Anyway, the therapist recommended a great sleepaway camp for Meir. She thought it would be really good for him to have a relaxed atmosphere in the summer and to get a new start socially where the kids don't know him and look down on him as a weak student and a kid with problems. And they actually work on social skills in this camp, too. I already spoke to the director."

"Sounds like an amazing opportunity," I said, wishing such a thing had been available when we were dealing with Yitzy. "What camp is this?"

"It's called Camp Chaverim. But…there's a slight problem."

I waited, holding my breath and feeling a fluttery sense of premonition.

"The tuition is $3,000 for one session."

I whistled loudly, my heart plummeting straight to my stomach.

"Do you think you and Tatty might be able to help us with this?" Michal asked, and I could picture her bright blue eyes staring straight into mine, pleading.

A weighty silence stretched between the two of us as a confused jumble of thoughts whirled through my mind. Three thousand dollars? But that's how much our new kitchen floor will cost! I've waited five years for this, five long years of watching the holes in the floor grow by the day, grimacing every time I sweep and notice another piece of the wood fraying. And finally, Moshe and I decided we would put in a new floor this year, and the contractor is actually scheduled to come on Wednesday with some samples. Would I have to shelve my long-awaited dream for my grandson's needs? Was that fair? Don't parents have needs, too?

"Ma?" Michal intruded on my silent reverie, and I realized I hadn't given her an answer.

"Let me talk with Tatty," I said. "Of course we'd love to help. The question is what we're able to do. I'll let you know soon, okay?"

As I hung up and balled my fists in frustration, I watched the dream of my new floor sprout wings and go flying through the open window and soar heavenward. I knew that somehow we would wind up giving the money to Michal. What doesn't one do for a child and grandchild? They're more important than a mere floor, right? But it's not just a floor; I'm embarrassed when we have company. And I'm tired of living like this, it's affecting my *simchas hachaim*. Besides, we had no one to turn to while we were raising our kids to help us with extras like this. We had to do everything on our own. So maybe it's okay to say no.

Michal will understand, won't she? She knows we struggle with money, and we help when we can. But what will she say if I tell her a regretful no, and then she comes over and sees a magnificent new kitchen floor? Something tells me she won't really get it, and then our relationship might be damaged forever… Can someone please tell me what to do? You sacrifice your whole life for your kids; does it ever end? Are you ever able to take care of your own needs?

Michal Speaks:

"Happy anniversary, Dovid. Can you believe it's been ten years already?" We sat together with cups of hot cocoa, reminiscing as we celebrated.

"Ten wonderful years. I couldn't have asked for a better wife and mother for our children, Michal."

"Maybe we need to call and thank our *shadchan* again. She really gave us the gift of life." These positive thoughts brought my mind to my greatest insecurity, my son. "But, Dovid, about being a wonderful mother, I just don't feel that any of the methods I've used with our other children work with Meir. It's almost as if he doesn't hear me or doesn't want to hear me. I get so scared when his behavior seems so out of control. I just can't help wondering what the future holds for him. He reminds me of…"

Dovid gave me a knowing look. "Don't torment yourself. Listen to me. You're a fantastic mother. You take parenting classes. You ask advice from experienced mothers. You work on yourself not to respond reactively, but in ways that are conducive to our children's learning. Since when are results in our hands? And what about all the various therapy appointments that you expended time and money on for the last couple of years? Knowing about our parents' tight finances, we tightened our belts and paid out of our own pockets. You gave up fancy jewelry to polish your living diamonds. And you must admit that Meir's tantrums have decreased."

"You're a phenomenal defense attorney to my harsh inner critic," I told him, "yet my heart isn't at peace knowing that he suffers and that he doesn't fit in socially with his classmates. His learning challenges affect his self-esteem and sometimes he just looks up at me with this confused look on his face as though he really doesn't understand what the world is asking of him."

"Michal, your intuition is usually on the mark, so let's make an appointment with the school tomorrow. Maybe they will have some helpful ideas." Dovid stood up and headed toward the counter, "Can I please taste a piece of that delicious looking cream cake you somehow managed to find time to bake?"

After I nodded, he cut us neat slices, a delicious treat for such a special milestone. As I ate the first bite, I resolved to contact the principal and see if he could help.

I came home a week later replaying the scene in my head of our meeting with the principal.

"Mr. and Mrs. Stern, thank you for your trust in our school and for your active cooperation. We believe that partnership between parents and teachers holds the key to student success. Although Meir has made significant progress academically and behaviorally, his recent comprehensive testing revealed a speech and language processing disorder. We'll notify the teachers so that we can individualize Meir's learning goals and provide two hours of remedial services each day.

"There's another idea that may be very helpful as well. A new camp opened that uses research-based methods to help children with challenges similar to Meir's. They have an excellent success rate. The only drawback is that it's quite expensive, as they have a very low therapist-to-student ratio. And at this point, unfortunately, there are no discounts available. I suggest you discuss this at home and contact me if you'd like me to write a personal recommendation for Meir. I truly think this would be an ideal fit for him and that he'd thrive in their stimulating environment."

I leaned back in the chair thinking hard. Dovid was doing the same.

"Dovid, are you thinking what I am thinking?"

"You know my father has been unemployed for years now," he said, defensive and misunderstanding me.

"I know. I was thinking of my parents. It's so hard to ask. My parents never even sent us to camp because there was never enough money to afford that luxury for so many children. We were allowed to earn our own money, but anything beyond food, shelter, and some clothing was considered a luxury. I always felt resentful when all of my friends went to camps and ate regularly in restaurants. It seems almost ludicrous or maybe satisfying on some primitive level to ask them to sponsor their grandson's camp. Yet, money continues to be so tight for them. Two siblings overseas, tuition, Yom Tov, weddings, bar mitzvahs… Now that we have to pay bills, I understand so much better, although the little girl in me still wants Mommy to come to the rescue. It is their grandchild, after all.

"Lately, Mommy has mentioned wanting to fix up their house," I continued. "None of us appreciate staying there, as it's looking more and more run down. Yet we all keep asking for help. If we can't go to our parents when we have needs, who can we approach?

"Dovid, how can I feel both entitled to ask and guilty at the same time? I'm so confused. Wouldn't Mommy and Tatty want Meir to have this opportunity? Aren't we the most important people in their lives? Isn't it wrong not to go to parents when we have needs? We'd want our children to always feel free to ask us!"

He nodded, listening.

"Okay, are you calling or am I calling? If this is the right thing to do, why is my heart pounding, my palms sweating, and my hands shaking?"

I picked up the phone and dialed Mommy's number, nerves bubbling inside of me. When she answered, I was barely able to speak. "Hello, Mommy, how are you, it's Michal speaking…"

2

NO PIZZA FOR ME?!

Mommy Speaks:

"Hi, Brachie! How was your day?"

I turned from my pots on this short *erev Shabbos* to give Brachie a smile as she walked into the kitchen. Picking up an empty pizza box, she looked at me questioningly.

"Is there pizza?" she wanted to know, her eyes looking hopeful.

"Afraid not, sweetie," I answered. "Nosson and Libby had some, and there's no more."

"How could you do that?" Brachie's voice was strident. "You know I love pizza! How could you get pizza and not save some for me?"

Breathless from extensive preparations since all of our

out-of-town children and grandchildren were visiting, I didn't really feel up to being my daughter's punching bag at the moment. Maybe another time. I was working so hard to make everyone comfortable with their food and lodgings, and now...

I sighed.

"It's a short *erev Shabbos*, Brach. And I made you lunch this morning. We got exactly enough pizza for the people who needed to eat. I didn't think you needed two lunches."

"It's not fair! You always give them the best things just because they don't live at home anymore. I don't count at all. Oh, no. Give me noodles and that's fine. But when they come, they get pizza."

I furrowed my eyebrows, unsure where this onslaught was coming from. Hadn't I just taken her out yesterday for a special ice cream date before all the kids came in? Was it ever enough, or would I always be found lacking?

"Why didn't you get me some?" she demanded, hands on her hips and eyes flashing furiously. "You never think of me."

Immediately my mental Rolodex rewound to our ice cream trip from yesterday, and then continued to play images of the countless things I've done for this child since she first appeared in this world.

"What do you mean?" I countered, moving over to slice tomatoes for the salad. "I made you pancakes the other day, drove you to play practice, got you ice cream... What exactly do you mean that I never think of you?"

"They're just more important since they're married and don't live at home," she snarled, placing special emphasis on the word married. "I don't count. I'm a nothing."

Clamping my lips shut so I wouldn't say anything I'd regret, I withdrew into a subdued silence, davening to Hashem that He should take the wind out of her sails. Tired and overworked, I really didn't feel up to a full-fledged teenage uprising at the moment. *But it just isn't fair*, I thought, dicing the green peppers and throwing them into the large salad bowl. Just when I'm working my hardest and trying my best to do everything for everyone, why is that the time to take aim and fire at Mommy for failing once again?

Brachie Speaks:

In a way, although I wouldn't tell Mommy (because I'd rather that she pick me up most of the time), the walk home from school is positive. It gives me a chance to air my thoughts. In some ways, I just love when my married siblings come to visit. The house is so lively and exciting and the table talk so interesting. My brothers-in-law are fun, and I wouldn't admit to anyone that I actually enjoy when they tease me. And the babies are adorable, even though I need to fight with Penina, my eight-year-old sister, for holding rights — absolutely ridiculous, if you ask me. But — now we are getting to the crux of the problem — no one does ask me!

When my married siblings are away, it's a chorus of "Brachie, do this," and "Oh, Brachie, can you just…?"

When they come, it's as if I become a second-class citizen. They have no responsibilities and are treated like royal visitors. Yours truly has much more work as a result, yet only gets to eat their scraps.

It really hurts. Mommy knows that pizza is my absolute favorite food in the whole world. What does having already eaten lunch have to do with pizza anyway? Sometimes the logic of parents is utterly befuddling.

I wish Mommy would understand that when they come and she expects so much more from me, I need more privileges instead of feeling like I'm back to being one of the little ones and practically being given a bedtime again.

On the one hand, part of me feels bad for Mommy. She wants to make a nice visit for her children and misses them when they're away, yet she works so hard the whole time they are here, she hardly gets to see them. I feel like a prop; I'm supposed to help make this picture-perfect visit. I wonder what is it about marriage that seems to take helpful, capable girls and turn them into couch potatoes when they visit their parents.

Hey, I just had an idea — maybe I should visit a *shadchan*, find a nice guy, and then I can also sit and visit while Penina does all the work. Oh, what a totally lovely picture. She's so spoiled. Mommy hardly asks her to do anything, and she can't do any wrong.

Seriously, my parents seem to misconstrue anything I say as rude or inappropriate, so even when I start out trying to just express my point of view, I get cut off, which makes me really angry. They just tell me to be grateful for all of my privileges and appreciate how few responsibilities I really have compared to when they were children. Isn't it a nuisance when parents do that? I know my mother had to clean half the house weekly because her mother was a widow and worked to support them, and her sister was never much help in the cleaning department. Maybe I take after Aunt Raizel, although now she seems to actually enjoy helping Mommy in the kitchen, even (gasp!) washing the dishes. Other than that flaw, Aunt Raizel is a lot of fun and seems to get my way of thinking. She never understood why I needed to choke down food I don't like because children are starving in Africa, either. And she thinks I'm very funny!

Maybe Aunt Raizel can help me with this situation. I do love my siblings and enjoy seeing them. But everything is so complicated. If only we could get a live-in maid to do all the work so we can just sit around and schmooze. And maybe Penina can go sleep at a friend's house for a couple of days.

■ ■ ■

IT WAS A GREAT IDEA to talk to Aunt Raizel, who happens to be a therapist. She didn't seem shocked at my outburst and really seemed to accept my feelings.

At first, I felt a bit funny picturing how "nerdy" it seemed to actually speak to a therapist. But then I told myself that this is my aunt and maybe she can really help me, and what my friends don't know won't hurt them, or me, for that matter.

Aunt Raizel listened carefully, and I could tell she understood. It was a relief to express my feelings without having to worry that I might hurt someone by doing so and then wallow in the guilt afterward, which is the absolute worst feeling in the world!

My aunt knows how much I love acting and asked if I wanted to do some role-playing with her. That actually sounded like fun, so I agreed. Besides, it's nice to have someone ask me what I want for a change. It beats being Brachie the prop.

She asked if she could be me and I could play my mother. This was becoming both interesting and a bit frightening at the same time. I agreed again, although a bit more tentatively this time. What did this unpredictable lady have up her sleeve?

Come on, Brachie, you trust her, remember? And you asked to speak with her, so get over it and stop behaving like a baby, especially if you don't want everyone else to treat you like one. Okay, boy she actually sounds like me. Listen to this:

"Mommy, I see you got pizza today. Do you mind if I ask you a favor? I really love pizza and it's hard to come home from a tough day at school to find the empty pizza crumbs sitting in the box. Would you mind keeping me in mind next time this happens, even if I already had a meal? You know I'm never too full for a yummy slice of my favorite food. Thanks, Mommy."

How do I think my mother would react to such a speech? Probably a lot differently than she reacted after the way I approached her. That was just the first part of our conversation. Aunt Raizel and I (in our new roles) went on to discuss older sisters getting married and how it affects the single ones at home. She really gave me food for thought, and as long as my friends were nowhere in the vicinity (I scanned the area first), I actually gave her a hug. She looked pleasantly surprised.

For some reason, this situation with my married siblings makes me see red, and I do lash out at my mother in a way that makes me feel like a worm afterwards. I am really going to try to enjoy all the good parts of this visit. And my sisters are really a lot of fun. Maybe, just maybe, they want to enjoy a break when they visit since it's a vacation for them from their regular load of housework and childcare.

Could that be what's going on here? Can I possibly be misinterpreting Mommy's desire to give them a break as not caring about my needs?

Maybe I need to take a walk more often… hey, how about a walk to the pizza shop!

Now that's an idea, and I will give my aunt the olives because she seems to be on another one of her endless new diets, although she doesn't let me use that word — she calls it a "lifestyle change."

A lifestyle change… Hmmm. Can I really work on communicating to my parents without sarcasm so they can focus on my feelings? Fortified with pizza (minus the olives), I feel energized and ready to try again.

3

CAN IT BE?

Nechama Speaks:

Can it be? Will I really hold a gift of new life in nine months' time, another precious miracle that Hashem has gifted us? How can I adequately thank HaKadosh Baruch Hu for His infinite kindness yet again?

Oh, but then I remember…the stain on my happiness that sends my joy into a nosedive. My dear and only sister, Hindy, has been married several years longer than I, and only has two children, while I, her younger sister, will soon have my fifth, *bli ayin hara*. Hindy has struggled with infertility over the years, and each pregnancy is accompanied by a great deal of difficulty and interventions, in both the physical and in the *ruchniyus* realm. How can I tell her my news and cause her more pain? Maybe I won't share the news yet; it's still early.

I wish I could give Hindy some of my fertility as a gift. Why, I wonder, does pregnancy come to me so easily that I don't have time to wonder and worry, while for her, there's anxious waiting, accompanied by fear that the small family she has will remain that way?

She probably thinks I'm oblivious to her pain, living in my own little bubble of baby happiness, while in truth, I drink from her bitter cup in large doses, almost as if it's happening to me. We're so close, and it's agonizing to watch her suffer. She and her husband are so good, so fine, so *ehrlich*; Hashem, in His infinite wisdom, knows why they have to suffer this excruciating *nisayon*. All I know is that it hurts me too, more than she will ever know. Because when you love someone, it hurts to see them in pain.

Just the other day, Hindy came over to visit with her two beautiful big boys, ages six and nine. They invited us to join them at the park. "Sure," I agreed. But then I had to nurse the baby, and her boys got really restless. When I thought we were finally ready to go, the baby spit up, and I had to change two outfits — his and mine. Then my toddler had a dirty diaper... "You know what?" Hindy finally suggested, gathering her boys and heading for the door. "We'll meet you there. These guys need to get out."

"Okay," I agreed, feeling almost guilty for being so consumed with my babies. *It's not my fault!* I wanted to say. But I winced as I glimpsed the pain in her eyes. Then, a few nights later, it happened again. Hindy called me and needed a recipe. The baby picked that moment to start screaming, so I couldn't talk.

"Can I call you later when things quiet down?" I asked.

"Sure," she agreed, but I heard the silence from her end of the line, and I sighed. Her home was already quiet for the night. Her boys were peacefully in bed, and she was free to pursue other venues. But I knew her secret wish and was keenly aware that she'd love to be so busy that she didn't have time to make a simple phone call.

Who's calling? Gulp, it's Hindy. I hope she won't hear anything in my voice that will give away my secret.

"Hi, Hindy, how are you? You're just coming from the doctor? Oh, I hope the new treatment works. I know Masha had something similar and it was successful. Yes, of course I'll daven for you. I always do, but I'll do more, of course… What? That must have been so awkward. It's the worst when people try to avoid you. Did they even say hi? Or pretend you weren't there? Ah-ha, I guess you're right that it doesn't make it easier. Well, Hindy, Hashem should answer our tefillos — soon, *b'ezras Hashem*. And Hindy," I continued, my heart hammering violently, "I have something to share with you…"

Hindy Speaks:

Growing up with just one younger sibling, I yearned to be the mother of a large, warm, and lively family. And while my sister and most of my friends were blessed with children on a yearly basis, I have two delicious boys who are growing older without a newborn cry to be heard.

I felt less worthy and undeserving of Hashem's blessings. I was certain that my jealousy disrupted the flow of blessing.

I cried, prayed, worked on doing more acts of kindness, and tried very hard to rejoice and participate in people's *simchahs*. Often, my efforts bore fruit, while at other moments they felt futile. When I visited neighbors on Friday nights, all the attention was geared to the babies, their feeding and sleeping habits, and their adorable antics. What could I contribute without sounding pitiful? Sure, I remember my baby waking up for feedings, four years ago. When we went to parks together, I'd offer to push other children on the swings as the arms of the other mothers were clearly occupied. And all the neighbors' children came to our house for baking parties, as the other mothers were busy caring for infants.

The most intense pain involved my younger sister, Nechama. Watching her cuddle her adorable infants and stammer and stutter, trying not to cause me pain before she put on maternity clothing yet again, felt excruciating. I knew my response was illogical. She didn't contrive this plan. I was the older sister. Throughout our childhood, I protected her and on some level — in my father's absence and my mother's lack of formal Torah education — felt like a quasi-parent.

Nechama was shy and reserved and I paved the way, which she followed appreciatively. How can I relate to her without embarrassment now that she's the mother of so many more children than I? Now that she possesses skills and experiences I don't, how can she consult me for my opinion? What do I know about juggling a new baby on a yearly basis while still valiantly attempting to care for the other children's needs? Is it possible that Nechama wants to ask for my guidance but because she perceives my agony, she doesn't dare? If I exuded serenity, maybe she would once again take counsel and value my sisterly perspective.

Yes, my head knows that Hashem gives each of us what we are supposed to have to best fulfill our purpose. Yet my heart still protests at the perceived unfair distribution of *berachos*. How can I appear peaceful if I'm angry at her, if I resent her being ahead of me? A part of me screams, "It's not fair! She's younger than I am! How could she do this to me?!"

Then, I feel ashamed. Can I only be a nurturing older sister from my secure place in the top row, and when that is threatened and usurped, my love is switched off? Am I really so shallow and superficial?

I coped by overachieving and preparing for my students till the wee hours of the night. I coped by giving each of my children loads of individual time so that even when my friends were free to chat at night, I didn't allow myself that luxury. I coped by trying to feel worthy. Slowly, I began to grow up and allowed my heart to absorb the truth that my brain understood. Tears still came readily each time my hopes were disappointed, yet the other part of me yearned to find meaning in the *berachos* I received. I have adorable children who need their mother. I have growing students anxious to internalize Torah lessons. Clearly, Hashem designed this challenge for me to grow and to abandon the constant comparison that sucked the joy out of every opportunity for gratitude. And a small voice whispered, *Do you think those on the other side of the fence don't have challenges? Be honest,* I told myself, *every situation contains real nisyonos and you have seen some with your own eyes. Do I choose to continue to live life with the mentality of "the grass is always greener" echoing in my thoughts and interrupting my enjoyment of each moment?*

Life isn't a race of how many babies one can produce in the shortest time. Life is a truly individualized contest of trying to be better each day in a real way. The fountains of love I feel for my sister and her children, who have become cherished nieces and nephews, are the source of great *nachas* that we share.

Once I came to that realization, I gave myself permission to love my life exactly the way it is. And, in a magnificent sign of *hashgachah*, when women came crying to me with similar stories of anguish, they felt comforted by my experience and we gave strength to each other. Then I knew that my head and my heart were one.

4

MATHEMATICALLY SPEAKING!

Mother Speaks:

The conversation started off innocently enough. Had I known how it would escalate, I would've put on a suit of armor. Kids these days; you just can't win.

Devorah came home from school, and we were eating together at the kitchen table.

"So, I want you to ask Mrs. Lieberman to switch me to the lower math class," Devorah told me, spearing her potato and looking me in the eye.

"Oh?" I said, somewhat surprised. "Why?"

"Because I can't do it!" Devorah's eyes flashed with anger and frustration. "I don't belong there!"

Looking at my straight-A student of a daughter, I felt sure she was capable of doing the work. Maybe pre-algebra didn't come as easily to her as other subjects, but with a little more effort, I had full confidence in her abilities to succeed. Flashbacks of my trying to help her here and there streamed through my mind, and I knew my assistance was useless; algebra was definitely not my thing. But I'd just attended the parent-teacher conferences, and her math teacher had assured me she was available to help students who were struggling, setting aside several periods a week when students could work with her. She'd also told me Devorah had improved since the beginning of the year, and currently had a B average.

"Devorah," I said, "have you approached your teacher to ask for help? She told me she has time."

"I don't want to do that!" Devorah exploded. "I just want to switch to the other class! Why can't you ever help me?"

Okay, Rachel, deep breath. She's just a teenager and doesn't mean to fling mud in your face… At least I don't think she does.

"But how can I ask Mrs. Lieberman to switch you before you even put in any effort? The first thing she's going to ask me is if you got help."

"Mommy." Devorah fixed me with an icy glare. "I can't do this math. I don't understand it and that's it."

"Sweetie," I replied, "I think you're very capable and you can do it — you just have to try harder or get some tutoring help. Going to the lower class is a cop out. Who said everything in life is easy? Try first, go to your teacher and—"

"I didn't ask you what you think I should do!" Devorah shouted. "I asked you to speak to my principal and get me out of this class!" She pushed her chair back and stood up. "You know what? I should've known you wouldn't be on my side. Never mind. I'll just go to Mrs. Lieberman myself. I don't know why I thought I could talk to you. Like you'd understand."

Tossing her ponytail over her shoulder, Devorah flounced out. I heard her door slam. Lifting a fork to my mouth, I noticed that my stir-fry was suddenly tasteless. Where had I gone wrong in this conversation? Oops! I hadn't empathized. I guess that should have been step one. Maybe I should've tried problem-solving together with her? But she didn't really want to problem-solve, she wanted me to go along with her pre-decided plan, and I didn't, because I didn't agree with it. Oh, well. I sighed. Maybe next time will go better.

Devorah Speaks:

Waves of anger wash over me. Mothers can be *so* frustrating. And, yes, though I don't like to admit it to myself, much less to her, I do feel guilty. We learn about the importance of honoring parents, and I ace all the tests in school, but then in the school of real life, she just pushes my buttons and I explode.

Sometimes, I don't feel like anyone understands what I go through. And I guess underneath all of this anger is sadness. When I was a little girl, I remember snuggling next to my mother when I felt sad, and she'd hold me and just seem to understand my needs without me saying a word. Now, even when I say many words, it feels like there's a huge wall between us and we're speaking two different languages.

Aren't mothers supposed to understand their children? She always says she knows me better than I know myself. So then she would know that ever since first grade I've been known to my classmates as an A student. Getting a B would lower my status and I'd be teased mercilessly because my classmates know how much I push myself to get on the honor roll every marking period. For her, a B may mean an improvement. For me, it feels like a failure, a failure to achieve the A everyone expects of me and that I expect of myself.

Also, my two older siblings went to the top seminary in Israel. How will it look if I have to go to a less-academic choice just because of this awful algebra? What's wrong with math anyway? Who designed this ridiculous language with X's and Y's that are supposed to balance the world with equality?

Mommy always said that everyone has her own talents. I can't sing, dance, act, or get into the really popular group in school. All I have is my straight-A average. That's all that makes me special, and I just can't afford to lose that. And when I finally plucked up the nerve to reach out to Mommy for help to let me escape this humiliation, she just wants me to endure it more. I feel dumb with this teacher, and it's too painful to sit there for even one more day.

Sometimes, I think that it's not about my feelings. Maybe Tatty and Mommy are embarrassed to have a child in the slower class. They're both prominent people in the community. Yes, that must be it — I'm an embarrassment to them.

5

HAKOL BESEDER

Daughter-in-law Speaks:

The time has finally come. We have four children, *bli ayin hara*, traveling is exhausting, and we're ready to make our own Sedarim and be *mekayeim* the mitzvah of *v'higadeta l'vincha*. I can picture it now; Sruli will light up when we focus all of our attention on him and the beautiful Haggadah he made in kindergarten. He loves sharing what he knows, and he'll get so much out of the Sedarim if we have our own. The twins, Chaya and Chavie, are already in first grade, and they'd benefit so much from a give-and-take on their level. And what bliss to be able to put

Yitzy to sleep in his own comfortable crib instead of the one at my in-laws where he screams and screams.

When we go to my in-laws, it's a mob scene. All my husband's siblings are there with their kids, and no one gets any quality attention. Of course it's beautiful for families to be together, but let's save that beauty for another time. The more I think about it, the more certain I feel that staying home would be so beneficial to every one of our kids. I just hope my in-laws understand.

I know my mother will understand; she raised her own large brood and is keenly aware of how much children need individual time and attention, especially when the mitzvah of the day is *v'higadeta l'vincha*. She also remembers how difficult traveling is with a horde of little ones and how intensely challenging it can be when kids are off schedule. Memories of last Pesach fill my mind... what a disaster! Sruli was either having tantrums or fighting with everyone all day every day of Yom Tov and *chol hamoed* just because he was tired! It was so unfair to him. And then he'd have to go into time-out when it really wasn't his fault. Chaya and Chavie were irritable and kvetching for the same reason, and I found myself desperately reaching into my toolbox to try to handle their moods, but it was exhausting! And people think going away for Pesach is a vacation?!

So it's clear to me the time has come for us to make our own Pesach. The real problem is that my in-laws live locally. If we say we're not up to making the long trip to my parents, that's understandable. But I don't think they'll get the other piece about our wanting to make our own Sedarim so we can focus on the kids and really give them what they need. So exactly how do we explain not coming to them? I think they'll take it as a personal affront; I know they will!

Honestly, their Sedarim drag out way too long. They do things at a snail's pace; the same *divrei Torah* and songs could be shared in half the time! We'd all get more out of the Sedarim if they ended at one in the morning instead of four — it's just too much. Also, even though we avoid the 12-hour car trip by going to them, we still have to pack everyone up, the kids still get off-kilter because of a different location and schedule, and…can't I just be home? Isn't that what being mature and married is all about, being old enough to run my own home and make my own decisions based on what I feel is best for my family? So why do I have this sense of impending doom about Yanky telling his parents we won't be coming this year? He said he's going to tell them tonight.

Hey, I think I just remembered a *shiur* I have to go to, and it starts at the same time that he's planning to make *the* phone call. I may even go early to help set up…

Mother-in-law Speaks:

Hello, Yanky, so nice to hear your voice! I was just going to call you. It's time to start planning the Pesach menus and write down everyone's favorites so all the *kinderlach* can know just how much Bubby loves them. You know, when I was young, I remember eating my Bubby's special Pesach sponge cake — it tasted of her love and sweetness. Zeidy and I were just discussing how much we look forward to having all of our children around the table. A taste of heaven!"

I was so excited, I was just gushing. But I rein in my excitement to allow Yanky to speak.

"So, Yanky, sorry I haven't let you get a word in edgewise, but it's such a treat to hear your voice. To what do I owe the honor of your call at this time of the evening?"

"Mom, I'm not sure it's such a good idea for us to go anywhere for Pesach…" He proceeds to explain something about *chinuch* and not wanting to make me feel bad, but he needs to put the kids first. I'm so upset I can't even think clearly. All I know is that I have to hang up before I explode at him. Doesn't he know how much this means to us?

"Yanky, I'm shocked and don't want to say anything I may regret. Can I talk to you after I discuss this with Zeidy? Okay, I'll call you back soon."

After a long discussion, I call him back. My heart is hammering, but I think I can get through this without yelling or crying. "Yanky, Zeidy and I talked…well, more like Zeidy talked and I cried. You and I have a close relationship and I want to be very honest about my feelings regarding your decision.

"Pesach and family are synonyms, inseparable concepts spiritually and emotionally. Pharaoh tried to sabotage family time and that's one aspect we celebrate with our freedom. Your children experience true generational tradition. Every Shabbos, they sit with their own nuclear family and you have the opportunity to inculcate whatever you want into their precious minds and *neshamos*. A few times a year, however, you compromise on what you can do for your children in exchange for the priceless gifts they receive from being part of a chain that extends for generations.

"Do you really want to deprive them of that gift that won't be around forever, not that I am trying to be morbid or anything like that? I understand the challenges of packing up all the kids and having them out of sync in a different setting or on a different schedule. But, Yanky, let's be honest, a Yom Tov schedule is different anyway and they'll be off schedule even in their own home. If there are particular problems that make it more difficult, why can't we sit down and problem-solve? There's nothing I wouldn't do for you and your precious family.

"Please discuss this again with Devorah. Bye, Yanky, have a good evening and…thanks for calling."

My heart is pounding so loudly, I'm waiting for the neighbors to knock and ask about the noise. The pain hurts so badly. It's not just that Pesach won't be the same and that it's a time to *shep nachas*, as hectic, wild, and crazy as it is when everyone is here under one roof. It goes deeper than that. I don't even want to voice that it feels like my children are placing their own comfort above that of their parents' enjoyment.

I never wanted to be one of those mothers who say, "After all that I did for you all these years…" Yet, what about working hard to give grandparents some joy in their older years? Is that negotiable just so the children may learn a bit more at a quieter table or not have the inconvenience of relocating for a few days? It's not like they have to travel far; we live twenty minutes away. And even if they reconsider, this hurts so badly. I thought they cherish these times as much as we do, and now that seems doubtful.

I must calm down. What would my dear friend and mentor, Sora Leah, advise me? She'd tell me not to let myself interfere with the relationship. That means I must take a deep breath and try very hard to see the world from the perspective of young parents. It's not that they don't love us or don't care. Okay, the tears are still there but the pounding is getting just a bit softer.

Uh oh, someone's knocking.

"Who is it?"

"It's Miriam from next door, we just heard loud pounding and wanted to make sure that everything is okay."

6

HURRIED AND HARRIED

Rivky Speaks:

"Hi, Mommy!" I breezed, trundling into my in-laws' home to prepare for my brother Baruch's wedding that evening. Breathless and tired after our long car ride, my husband and I herded the kids inside, enjoyed my mother-in-law's delicious and thoughtfully prepared snack, and ran upstairs to get ready.

"Yoni, here's your tie!" I called, trying desperately to fix the tie he insisted on unclipping every time I got it straight. *Whose idea was it that a three-year-old should wear a tie, anyway? I'd like a word with them.*

"Shira!" I smiled and held up a gown for my one-and-a-half-year-old. She took one look and tore off in the opposite direction, exploding with a loud giggle. I moaned and started the chase. Normally I'd find this amusing, but since the clock was ticking, it was somewhat nerve-racking. *How much time do we have anyway?* I looked at my watch for the tenth time in as many minutes.

"Aha! Caught you!" I gave an exuberant victory cry, but Shira wouldn't be defeated. Tilting her head away from me, she swung her arms with abandon, while I tried vainly to pull the gown over her flailing, protesting body.

Oh, my sheitel! I touched my snood-covered head and gasped. *I'm supposed to be at the sheitelmacher in ten minutes. I guess Hashem can make miracles. Breathe, Rivky, breathe.*

Shoving our squalling three-month-old into my bewildered husband's arms, I grabbed the car keys and zoomed off to my appointment. Desperately urging the car through the winding streets of the neighborhood, I gritted my teeth when traffic slowed my journey. *Baruch's getting married tonight. Little Baruch...* My heart swelled with memories, fond memories of growing up with my terrific younger brother, when suddenly — *BEEP*! I slammed on the brakes and decided I'd better focus on the road. Best to leave thinking for later.

At last we were ready, picture perfect, and in a dazzling, flashing dream, my little brother, Baruch, became a husband. We beamed, we danced, the wedding was magnificent…and then it was over. Piling back in the car, we returned to my in-laws' and collapsed on the couch. My mother-in-law was waiting for us, looking like she wanted to spend some time with us and hear all about the *simchah* and its highlights. *That makes sense*, I thought, *but not now. Not after a day like today. After all, marrying off a little brother is a lot of work*! Physically and emotionally drained, I wanted nothing more than to spend a few quiet minutes talking with my husband before dissolving into a welcome sleep.

"Good night, Mommy," I said, pecking her on the cheek and starting up the stairs, beckoning my husband to follow. And I wondered, *Is that a tear running down Mommy's cheek? I wonder what happened...*

Mommy Speaks:

Okay, Esther, slow down and make a list... Greek yogurt for Rivky, kiddy yogurt for the baby, ingredients for all of Avromi's favorites, schnitzel, stuffed cabbage...

Esther, stop it. It's not Yom Tov, and they'll be so busy running around for this *chasunah* and *sheva berachos* that just an assortment of filling snacks will add the right touch.

I'm so excited to see them. I must call Sharon and tell her. She's such a wonderful friend and so sensible too.

"Hi, Sharon. You won't believe who's coming for three whole days, and not in the middle of a hectic Yom Tov. They're coming at a time when we can just sit and schmooze for hours. Oh, the sheer bliss just to imagine it! I'm dancing in the kitchen — good exercise, right?

"Why are you telling me to calm down and have realistic expectations? Of all people, I thought you would be so happy for me. Okay, I guess no one is perfect. I'm hanging up now to get the house ready and buy their favorite CD."

Maybe I should stock up on toiletries also, as it's so easy to forget important items when packing with young children. Next item on the to-do list: cancelling all my appointments for three days. After all, what's a bit of money compared to the *nachas* of my dear children? Each moment with them is a treasure!

"Here they come! Abba, they're here! Come in, *kinderlach*, so wonderful to see you! Have a delicious bite to eat and then I'm here at your service, ready to help with anything you need."

"Mom, don't you have clients now?"

"Don't worry, I cancelled them so we could spend quality time together. How often do I get the privilege of seeing you? Fully available and at your service; just say the word."

I don't usually drink caffeinated coffee at this hour but I want to be wide awake for this long-awaited talk. It's so important to be there for your children just as a listening, nonjudgmental ear so they can share their full range of emotions.

"Hello, welcome home, you look like glowing newlyweds yourselves. Yes, of course I'm still awake, I was just counting the moments until you returned.

"Was it a beautiful *chasunah*? Come, sit down, and let's hear all about it."

They exchanged a quick glance between them. It appeared they were way too drained to sit down and review the highlights with me. I valiantly attempted to cover the disappointment that must have been written all over my face. The fact that I had been longing for this moment didn't diminish the difficulty of the task. I took a cleansing breath and turned to my children.

"Yes, yes, you need to be well rested, to get your strength back after all this excitement. We'll talk another time. Oh, of course I understand — sleep well, *kinderlach*, good night."

7

WHAT'S THE BIG DEAL?

Blimi Speaks:

"Have you seen the newest diet?" Mindy, my neighbor, greeted me with a wide smile in the supermarket, pointing to the row of neatly stacked diet shakes and snacks, all sporting a good *hechsher*. Was it my imagination, or was she looking at the snacks in my cart with a superior shake of her head? "It's amazing, guaranteed to show results in just twenty-one days or your money back," she continued, seemingly oblivious to my reddening face. I watched her place the products in her cart, and then look back at me with questioning eyes, wondering if I would follow suit.

My blood rose to a rapid boil as I internalized her not-too-subtle hint. Yes, I had put on thirty pounds in a relatively short span of time. Stress can do that to people. How dare she assume I was unaware of what was going on with my own body, and that she had all the answers while I was enveloped by the darkness of ignorance? Just because I had more flab didn't mean a lack of brain cells. Who knew? Maybe my mind had gained weight in the process, too; that could account for some of those pounds, hmmm?

"Thanks for letting me know," I replied coolly, purposely bypassing the display and moving forward to continue my shopping in a different aisle.

"Can you believe what she said to me?" I seethed aloud later, pouring my wounded feelings into Zalmy's listening ears. "What a chutzpah!"

Zalmy cocked his head and shrugged his shoulders. "What's the big deal?" he said. "Why do you have to let her comments get to you?"

Blinking back stinging tears, I turned away so Zalmy wouldn't see my devastation at his callous response. Who else can you turn to for affirmation and comfort if not your husband? I needed empathy and reassurance that I was still beautiful, no matter what size I wore. Yet Zalmy had totally dropped the ball.

Come to think of it, I fumed, furiously attacking a pile of dirty dishes with hot sudsy water, *that's his mantra, so why am I surprised? He's often insensitive to my needs for emotional support, and instead of commiserating with me or validating my pain, he blithely tosses out his "What's the big deal?" comment and expects me to just snap out of my rut.* Ramming a clean glass down into the drainer, I was startled when it cracked, leaving sparkling shards all over the counter. Great. Just great. I'd better clean it up before someone gets hurt and it really becomes a big deal.

Sometimes I ask Zalmy to get me a specific item from the store, which is on his way home from work, and he comes home without it.

"It wasn't on sale today," he explains, tossing bags of all sorts of groceries I didn't need for this week's menu onto the floor.

How often have I asked him to leave my night table clear of his things so I can have my own little space beside my bed? As it is, we have a small room in a small house, and I don't have adequate space to call my own. All I want is a little corner where I know I can reach for my keys, book, and glasses without having to sift through his junk. Yet time after time, when I bring this matter to his attention, I'm accused of making a big deal out of nothing. And time after time, I find his ties, keys, glasses, or receipts tossed on top of my night table, and I'm forced to sift until I find my belongings.

I've tried bringing it to his attention in a calm, gentle manner. I've tried not greeting him with the request, making sure to serve him a nice supper first and ask him about his day. Nothing works. "Just let it go," he tells me, and I simmer in silence.

Should I let it go? Will he never change? How exorbitant is the price for *shalom bayis*? Does it mean I have to always give in on every issue? But then I feel stepped on and uncared for and wonder, *don't my needs matter*? Yes, each thing by itself may seem small. But if you take enough small things, they fill a large space. And as the years have gone by, there's a large space in my heart filled with anger and resentment and loneliness.

Maybe I'll try that diet after all. As long as Mindy's nowhere around. After all, what's the big deal?

Zalmy Speaks:

Sometimes I wonder if men and women studied language in different schools and learned different meanings for the same words. My wife, an otherwise intelligent woman, relays an incident to me that clearly disturbs her. Like any caring husband, I immediately drop everything else and give her my undivided attention. No multitasking or partial attention taking place here. She's clearly hurt by some comment expressed by a less than tactful friend. So I go the time-honored way of any good spouse, and attempt to fix the situation. Isn't that why she shares the event with her loyal and capable husband?

Yet, she then turns to me with anger and disdain as though I didn't understand the incident. So I patiently explain again that the best solution is to forget about it. It's no big deal.

I wouldn't tell her this and certainly wouldn't risk her reading this, but her disdain hurts me. I work hard taking care of the family. I give her time and attention, I try to fix all her problems. And on any given day, all I receive is a litany of complaints.

I spend time shopping for her, and she mentions the groceries I didn't purchase. I shut off my phone and give her attention; she uses this time to complain about my lack of attention to the children. No matter what I do, it just feels that I can't get it right with her. I put on this strong, masculine front, yet inside I feel so inadequate. I withdraw into my study to protect our connection, which I see withering away before my eyes.

At work, when I put on my confident voice, I receive respect. People ask me questions and appreciate the definitive response, which takes a weight off their shoulders. My style seems to work well at my job and my strengths are appreciated. Yet, every man knows that in the absence of respect from his wife, that confidence is merely a façade, an empty shell.

I don't know what to say to her anymore that will be appreciated. When her friend hinted to her that a diet might be a good idea, I simply avoided the weight issue. How could I risk telling her that our affection goes beyond appearance? Any time I've tried a comment of that nature, she's simply grabbed a tissue and looked at me with teary eyes clearly waiting for something, but no one told me my lines. That whole topic seems sensitive and off-limits. The truth is that my wife looks lovely to me, but I don't feel safe saying my true thoughts.

Could I even dare telling her how it feels to walk on eggshells, never knowing if my words are what she expects or needs? It feels way too risky to even try sharing my vulnerable side with her. Perhaps, in addition to the other flaws she already perceives, that would just make her see me as weak and less of a man.

So, where does this leave us? We're trapped in a pattern of two people who clearly need emotional closeness yet continue to miss the opportunity of providing that safe haven for each other.

Is there anyone who can teach us a common language so we can reach the secure closeness we both really want?

8

FORLORN AND FORGOTTEN

Miri's Mother Speaks:

"Mommy, can you check your email?" Miri asked the second she came home from school one Friday afternoon.

The pleading in Miri's eye compelled me to stop dicing and chopping, even though it was a short midwinter *erev Shabbos*. I took a quick detour and checked my computer.

"No, honey, sorry. There's nothing special there."

"Are you sure?" Miri's eyes looked puzzled. "Estie, Shiffy, and Rena all said their mothers got emails about Shoshie's birthday party. It's on Sunday."

"I'm sorry, sweetie," I said. "Maybe it will still come. Or maybe she doesn't have my email address."

Miri shrugged and went back to eating her snack. But I could see that her thoughts were focused on the party.

This scenario repeated itself the moment Havdalah was finished, and several times on Sunday morning. But at this point there was more than confusion reflected in Miri's eyes. There were hurt feelings and glittering tears.

"I'm bored," Miri complained at lunchtime on Sunday. "And there's no one to play with, because" — she paused and sniffed — "all of my friends are at Shoshie's party."

I quietly picked up the cordless. *I'll just go to my bedroom and make a quick call*, I thought. *After all, Miri's only eight. I'm sure Shoshie's mother won't mind having one more child if she knows how much it means to Miri.*

"Mommy, what are you doing?" Miri's eyes narrowed suspiciously. "Are you calling Shoshie's mother?"

"Uh, I was thinking about it," I admitted, feeling like I'd been caught with my hand in the cookie jar.

"Don't."

I reluctantly put the phone down, but I got the message. Yes, she wished she could go to the party, but only if she was wanted.

"This is really hard." I kissed the top of her downturned head and put my hand on her shoulder. "You feel left out." Miri lifted watery eyes and gazed into mine, revealing a broken heart.

"I thought she was my friend," she said.

"I know." I paused, my presence and demeanor exuding empathy. "I still wonder if they didn't have my email address. Or, here's another possibility. Maybe her mother told her she could only invite a few girls and have a small party."

The afternoon wore on, and Miri's ready smile and carefree

attitude remained shadowed. She agreed to come with my husband and me for a walk to the duck pond. We brought her scooter and our leftover Shabbos challah. But even the swarms of ducks enjoying the challah failed to keep a smile on her lips; she was definitely mourning. She scooted along the trail, her lips set in a determined frown, her eyes shuttered. And I watched her, wishing I could wipe away her pain.

By late afternoon, Miri found a friend to play with, and her mood picked up. But the tears were back when I said Shema with her that night.

"I'm so sorry," I murmured, giving her a good, long hug. "You're still upset about this, aren't you?" She cried in our embrace, and I lay down next to her until she fell asleep.

"You know," Miri told me the next day, "a lot of girls went to the party. Even more than I thought."

Ouch. I wish she didn't know that. But I guess you can't expect eight year olds to keep this type of thing quiet. I still wonder if it was a mistake, or if I should have called Shoshie's mother from a different room, and then told Miri that the email came… So much for 20/20 hindsight. Yet, now that it's over, I know these types of experiences build our spiritual muscles. Hard as it was, hopefully Miri will file it away and grow to become a more compassionate person.

"Mommy, can I please have a birthday party this year? Everyone is doing them and it's so much fun, please…?"

"Shoshie, let me speak to Abba and get back to you. Remember, we make decisions by thinking about what's best for you, not by what "everyone" does. And I'm not sure how we can possibly invite your whole grade — that's forty-five girls."

"Oh, Mommy, no one invites the whole grade anymore. That's so last year. Everyone knows it's just not done, and most girls get invited to at least some parties. Our gym teacher told us we have to be tougher and not get insulted so easily. She doesn't like when we cry, not one bit. So I'm sure everyone will be just fine." She looked at me with her arms akimbo, sure her logic would win out. Something still didn't feel right.

"Shoshie, something isn't sitting right with me here and I'll think about it and talk to Abba. Your feelings are certainly very important to me; however, how do we know that the girls who aren't invited and then hear about it won't be very hurt? You know Hashem cares very much how we treat each other."

I decided my husband would have good insight on the issue. "Abba, Shoshie wants a birthday party this year and apparently, according to our eight-year-old resident sociology expert, one no longer needs to invite the whole grade as 'everyone' understands that with the recession, choosing only some girls seems an acceptable option. Of course, I'll double check this with the principal but, assuming she has her facts correct, what do you think?"

"First of all, I can predict that my dear wife's heartstrings are tugging at her very tightly, worrying that nobody's feelings get hurt. Did I get that right? Great, can I please have the funds you would have handed to your life coach for that brilliant insight?" He laughed loudly, dispelling much of my tension.

"Okay, thanks for the laugh. But, seriously, how do we balance Shoshie's needs for a party with the very strong possibility that by excluding some girls, we're causing significant pain, not to mention potential loss of friendship?"

"Listen, of course we don't want to hurt people. I think we need to trust that mature adults understand that there are limits in these kind of activities. Knowing Shoshie's social challenges, preventing her from having the chance to participate might not be in her best interest. What did the principal say?"

"She said that in a school of this size, parents can't be expected to invite all girls, and that by inviting just a small group and not sending invitations in school, the girls need to learn to deal with disappointments. And parents and teachers can help our girls learn these coping tools. Just like you were saying. How do you manage to think so clearly without your heart confusing the issues?" I was always impressed by his levelheadedness, whereas sometimes my emotions got in the way.

He smiled, and then said, "So we'll tell Shoshie there are to be no invitations distributed at school to do our best to spare the feelings of the girls who aren't invited. We'll also limit Shoshie to a maximum of five girls from each class so even if other girls do learn of this party, they'll realize it was only a small group who participated. Thirdly, we'll remind her not to talk about it in school. Fourthly, you need to relax and let Shoshie choose her five friends from each class, instead of you choosing for her."

"How did you know I was thinking of Miri and her mother, and worrying about their sensitivities?"

"We need to empower Shoshie to choose her close friends if this is to be a healthy social experience for her. We shouldn't force her to invite Miri as one of the girls in her inner circle. Remember, this party is about Shoshie's needs, not about our social choices."

"If you're logically right, why am I picturing Miri sobbing into her pillow with her mother rubbing her back and wondering what kind of parents exclude eight-year-olds from birthday parties? Anyway, I'll take out the mixer and start baking. But why don't I feel more excited about this birthday party?"

9

PORCUPINE QUILLS

Malkie Speaks:

I really relate to porcupines. There's something about a well-aimed barb from my mother-in-law, may she live and be well, that sets my quills from supine to upright. We had the dubious pleasure of hosting her recently, and the memory of her oft-related speech still makes me bristle, even though she is, once again, with Hashem's kindness, safe, well, and a plane ride away.

My husband is a *rebbi*, a teacher par excellence. He's knowledgeable and proficient in his field, a veritable *chinuch* expert after spending thirty years in the classroom. We were both recently honored by the day school; Shalom — my husband — for his devoted years of service, and me for my years of volunteer work on behalf of the school. That's what brought my mother-in-law to our home.

"He could've been anything, Malkie," my mother-in-law began, and I heaved an inward sigh. I knew where this was going, and I nodded, wishing I still had a young baby whose wail would propel me away.

"He has such oratory gifts, and he's so smart! He was accepted to Columbia. I'll only say it once (*in this conversation, right, Mom?*), Malkie, but what a shame. Why, if he'd finished his law degree, he would have had it made. Dad built up the firm from scratch and established a whole clientele. He was respected and loved. People used to call him any time, day or night. Stevie could have stepped right into his shoes (*I thought they wear a different size*) and taken over the entire business. They would have been standing in line for him!"

And she shook her head ruefully, question marks dancing in her eyes at the incongruity of her dreams and real life.

I knew better than to argue, but those quills were poised.

"But, Mom, this is what he wanted. Don't parents want their children to be happy and fulfilled?"

"Well, yes, of course."

"So then what's the problem?"

"Oh, I don't know." She sighed emotionally, sliding a beautifully manicured hand through her perfectly coiffed hair. Her gold jewelry glinted as the sunlight hit it, and I studied her, simultaneously pitying her for her shallow values, while at the same time, wishing I could penetrate to her core and change her views.

"He could have been so successful (translation: rich). But," another sigh, "he became religious and married young. (*Right. It's all my fault. If he hadn't met me, perhaps he would have followed the trajectory of your dreams.*) I thought he'd go off to college, but instead, he went to Israel, dated briefly, and said he's getting married.

"'In how many years?' we asked him." She continued the saga, and I restrained myself from blurting out the familiar lines. "'Two months,' he told us. It was a good thing I was sitting down, Malkie. Oh, well. Life doesn't always turn out the way you want it to, does it?"

"No, Mom," I agreed, thinking of certain children who've caused me pain with their lifestyle choices. "It really doesn't."

As long as we're wishing for fairy tale endings, I wouldn't have minded supportive in-laws who embraced our way of life, though different from theirs, and showed me I'm the daughter they always dreamed of welcoming into their family.

"So, Malkie, I'm glad I came for him," she told me as I brought her to the airport on the day she left. "He only has one mother. I had to come, don't you see? How could I not?"

"But, Mom," I finally protested, voicing the pain of my inner child, "didn't you come for me, too?"

Both of my parents died many years ago, and it seems that a child, even when grown, never loses the longing for her parents.

"Oh, but you had so many people," she replied, brushing off my yearning like a piece of lint on her fur coat. "You didn't need me."

So many people? You mean my one and only brother and my, I mean *our*, children, who traveled in for both of their parents? Why can't there ever be unconditional love, even after thirty years? Would it have hurt to say that you came for both of us? And that you were proud of our accomplishments?

Mom Speaks:

I know some people advise that when your children are adults, keep your mouth closed and your wallet open. Yet, as a mom who really cares about her family, there are certain things just too painful to observe quietly. Let's take my son, for example. Not just because he's my son. Everyone says he's brilliant, analytical, classy, and an incredible orator. I can just close my eyes and picture him successfully winning case after case in the courtroom as he masterfully shreds his opponent's arguments to crumbs. He had received a scholarship to an Ivy League university, which was happy to hold his spot when he left to study in Israel for a year. He convinced them that studying Talmud would only sharpen his analytical skills, and they accepted that. Do you see what I mean about his persuasive skills?

I know we can't rewrite history. I know he refused the scholarship and felt fulfilled when he became religious and decided to marry his sweet wife when she was only eighteen. It was very hard then and it still is. There are so many lifestyle differences and so many rules that don't allow them to participate fully in our family gatherings. To be honest, I cover up that pain, but it still hurts. It's almost as though my child rejected the way of life we taught him and chose something totally different. Yet, if not for my worry about them, I would continue to hide my disappointment. Sometimes, it feels as though he was my baby just yesterday, yet I know that my long-term memory seems in sharper focus than my short-term memory. What do I hope to accomplish by rewinding their life story back thirty years?

I guess I really worry about their finances. They have a large family, and although beloved in their community — and I do have the most adorable grandchildren and great-grandchildren — it's so hard to see them struggle. I want to convey to them that I won't be here forever to support their way of life, and that my son needs to step up and support his large family. So although in the past my wallet has been open wide and I never was much good at the closed mouth part, now I just feel a bit reluctant to continue giving. Is my generosity doing him a disservice? Perhaps reminding my talented son about his gifts could push him to go back to school and get a more lucrative profession. Many people return to school and make career shifts at his age…and he still looks so young and handsome, everyone says so!

For some reason, though, whenever we have these conversations, my daughter-in-law gets so defensive. I'm not trying to attack, so why does she always seem to be defending herself against me? Doesn't she realize I love her? Why, I'm always bragging about my daughter-in-law who raised a double-digit family.

I'm still old-fashioned enough to believe that it is my son's job to support her, and she has worked so hard raising all these lovely children. She then makes these irrelevant comments about kids choosing their professions and finding fulfillment. What about dollars and cents? It costs a lot to provide for children. And the cost of living doesn't go down either. Sometimes, when I hear her speak, she sounds like the starry-eyed, impractical eighteen-year-old who captured my son's heart so many years ago. She's a smart girl. Hasn't she learned that dreams are nice, but that living costs money?

And, yes, what if the time comes when we can no longer help them? What if we can't afford to give them money because we incur the expenses that come with old age? Maybe they don't realize that the way of nature is for parents to pass on, and then we will no longer be able to help them. Even I know that the Torah doesn't say one must be poor to be observant.

I wish my daughter-in-law would understand the concerns I have for their future and financial security. Maybe I'll try to share my opinions just one more time. No one can ever say that I give up easily. Maybe my orator of a son didn't only inherit his brilliant skills from his father's side. What do you think?

10

KOALAS – HERE WE COME

Esther Speaks:

"Australia?! Yosef, I know you've wanted to take the next step for a while, and the salary sounds like we can live with a bit more peace of mind. Visualizing palm trees and the ability for our children to enjoy the outdoors every day sounds like a dream." Yet, if there's so much blessing in this opportunity, why is my stomach so tightly contracting? And why are the tears threatening to spill out in torrents?

"Esther, thank you for standing by my side and encouraging me. I know it must be beyond painful to think about leaving your mother and moving so far away. This is a joint decision. If it's too much to ask, we'll find another option."

"Mommy always said that if Daddy were alive, she would've followed him to the ends of the earth. She probably didn't realize she would have to eat her words one day. Yet she taught me that my place is by your side." Thinking about this made me feel more certain about this decision.

"Esther, let's do what we usually do when there's a significant decision. Let's ask *daas Torah* and accept the *rav's* guidance about this decision and its impact on Mommy. And remember, the *kollel* provides yearly trips to America, which we can utilize fully so Mommy can enjoy her precious grandchildren. If it makes you feel any better, by the way, I love Mommy too, and I'll also miss her."

"Thanks. Let me call Sora. She helps me see the big picture without being overwhelmed by emotions." I picked up the phone and prayed that my dear friend would answer. Her voice on the other line made me sigh with relief.

"Hi, Sora. How are you? What's new? Oh, same old, same old, except Yosef was just accepted to a *kollel* in Australia and my heart is breaking and feels torn between loyalty to my mother and to my husband. Yes, you heard correctly. Oh, Sora, what am I going to do? The guilt is overwhelming, whatever I do! It feels like a lose-lose. Either I cause pain to my mother, who's suffered tremendously throughout her life, or I disappoint my husband and interfere with the pursuit of his dreams. Our rabbi said we'll only see positive outcomes if we go away for Yosef's growth in Torah. My head may know that, but my heart is breaking."

"Esther, have you spoken to your mother yet?"

"No, I can't bring myself to call her. My stomach feels so tight, it reminds me of my most painful contractions."

"Take a deep breath. You're a wonderful person, and you love to please everyone and make them happy. It's really hard for you to inflict pain."

"That's right. Yet some decisions, by their very nature, involve hurting at least one person. And these are two of the most important relationships in my life."

"It must be incredibly difficult for you. Esther, can you find any benefit in this challenge? You often say that Hashem only gives us tests for our growth."

"Maybe I'll have to find other creative ways to reach out to my mother that I wouldn't have done while living close by. Maybe supporting my husband's dreams will help him grow in ways far beyond what he can achieve here. Maybe the unity Yosef and I will attain will create a more secure home environment for our children."

"You're doing so well. How are those contractions now?"

"Definitely quieter and I'm breathing more deeply. Sora, how can I thank you?"

"Isn't that what friends are for? This is tough. But I've never seen a tough situation stop you from proceeding with optimism and purpose. I noticed you didn't mention the possibilities of your own individual growth and developing your gifts. You've always dreamed of teaching high school. Maybe doors will open there too. And one more thing. Call your mother and have that conversation. I have no doubt she wants you to be at your husband's side." I hung up with much of my confusion and guilt resolved. I knew that once I spoke to my mother, I'd be able to move forward.

"Yosef, what did the *kollel* say about bringing our furniture? And can you get me a few numbers of women who live there so I can find out about schools and lifestyle expectations and maybe some job possibilities?"

"Looks like I have my happy wife back. Hashem will help us,

and I know this will be good somehow for all of us."

"Thanks for understanding my challenge and being patient with me. And can you call the travel agent and book our first trip back? I know that seems funny before we even get there. Yet just knowing we have a date to see Mommy again may help this transition. I'm calling Mommy now to share the news. Daven for me that this goes well." I dialed the number, hoping that my newfound positivity would make this easier, "Hi, Mommy…"

Mommy Speaks:

"Oh, hi, Esther, how are you? How're the kids?"

I was washing dishes when my eldest daughter called, but decided to take a break and relax on the couch while we schmoozed.

Living in Philadelphia while my two married daughters live in Cleveland is challenging, so I try to keep our phone call times sacrosanct. I've been a widow for nearly twenty years, and the girls are all I have.

"You have some news for me? Okay, I'm all ears. You're moving?! Where to? Australia?! Why not the moon? That may be closer. But," I could hardly choke the words out, "why on earth are you going there?"

"Yosef found a *kollel* he likes there. For a long time he's been searching for a growth opportunity that focuses on learning slower and more deeply than what's available here. It's a perfect opportunity."

After the silence had stretched uncomfortably long between us, Esther ventured a tentative, "Ma? Are you there?"

"Sort of," I said quietly. "You know, as much as I don't want you to move overseas and limit the time we see each other even more than it is already, I have to tell you something. If Daddy were still here..." I paused, swallowing the lump that just formed in my throat. "If Daddy were still here," I repeated, "I'd follow him to the ends of the earth. That's what a wife is supposed to do, support her husband. So, much as I don't want you to go...are you sure you can't find a *kollel* any closer where Yosef will *shteig*? Ah, you've looked everywhere... Well, then," I had to pause again; that lump was growing into a mountain, "I give you my blessing. You're doing the right thing."

"Oh, Mommy!" Esther cried out, and I reached for some tissues as tears cascaded down my cheeks. "This is so hard. I don't want to move so far away. But Yosef's been looking for so long and this *kollel* is exactly what he's been looking for. It's such a fantastic opportunity. And we'll come in the summer to visit before we go, okay? I love you..."

"A visit will be terrific!" I fought like a valiant soldier to inject enthusiasm into my voice. "That will be something to look forward to."

Our conversation veered to the kids and their antics, and I heard myself laugh at appropriate moments. But my mind was far away.

Australia? I stared blankly at the phone once our call was over. *When will I see her again?* I don't have money for that kind of trip. I can barely afford to pay my bills on my small secretary's salary. *How does a mother say good-bye to her daughter?* Even though they'd already booked their first trip back, I still felt uneasy. *Who knows how long they'll be able to continue making trips back to the States?* Well, at least there's the phone. I'm going to call AT&T and find out how much it costs to call Australia.

"How much?" Aghast, I hung up the receiver and burst into a fresh gale of tears. So I won't even be able to call her very often either; it costs a small fortune! Not only that, but there's a fourteen-hour time difference! Oh, Hashem — don't I have enough challenges in my life? My husband is gone and has been for a lifetime, I don't have money, which makes everything so much more difficult, and now Esther is leaving me. How will I cope? *Why did I tell her she has my blessing? Can I retract? No, Judy, you did the right thing. A mother is supposed to let her daughter spread her wings and not burden her with guilt.*

But if it's the right thing, why is it so hard?

11

MEET YOUR NEW GRANDSON

Stepmother Speaks:

"Meet your new grandson!" flashed on my cell phone screen alongside a magnificent picture of a beautiful new baby boy.

"Mazal tov!" I told the friend sitting beside me, as I stared at the picture in wonder. "Chaim and Shaindy had a boy!"

"Mazal tov!" She hugged me, and I grabbed my pocketbook and prepared to leave. Who had patience to sit through a lengthy *sheva berachos* when our long-awaited *simchah* had finally arrived? My heart danced, it sang, it exulted — our *tefillos* of several years had been answered! *Hodu LaHashem ki tov*! I must call everyone, the children, my sister, my in-laws, our close friends. I longed to reach through the phone and kiss the silken cheek of our family's newest member, and how I wanted to share in this poignant and precious moment.

I paused for an emotional moment to reflect. How much effort it took for us to reach this sublime moment! Allow me to explain. Chaim and his siblings became my children in a unique and special way. When Chaim was ten, I married his widowed father, becoming what the world disparagingly calls a stepmother. Disregarding the negative connotation, I wholeheartedly embraced him and his sisters as my children, determined to become their mother. It took years of patience and love, monumental effort, and rivers of privately shed tears, but we finally breached the chasm that separated us. By the time Chaim left for yeshivah at fifteen, he was finally calling me Ima, and my heart rejoiced. As the eldest, Chaim set the tone. Once he accepted me as his mother, his sisters followed suit.

But enough journeying back in the past, we have a trip to prepare for! So with Hashem's help, it will be a Wednesday *bris*, I calculated. Maybe we should stay for Shabbos?

I bounced the idea off Chaim, awaiting his reaction. Surely he'd want us there to share in this beautiful time.

"Well, Shaindy's parents will be here, and we're all going to her brother's so we can be together for Shabbos."

Ah. So we're not wanted. Could it be because, after all is said and done, I'm still only a stepmother? After all these years, has the barrier I thought we'd overcome returned to haunt me? Or are we really wanted, and perhaps I misunderstood? Confusion whirled within me, so I consulted with my sister (it comes in handy to have a mental health counselor in the family) as to the best way to make my proposal.

And after speaking to her, this is what I said to Chaim:

"We just want you to be happy. Tatty and I will come in for the *bris, im yirtzeh Hashem*, and if you'd like us to stay for Shabbos, fine. If it's not the right time, and you and Shaindy need privacy, that's fine, too. We'll just slip in and out." *From across the country, mind you.* "Be honest, please, and let us know what you want. It's whatever's good for you."

It took a day of silence for me to infer that they didn't want to tell us straight out not to come, but *hameivin yavin*. We needed to book our tickets, and I still wanted absolute clarity before making the final decision. Later in the day I found that my son had indeed responded, and yes, it would be better to just slip in and out. I couldn't help but wonder; would he have rejected me if he were my flesh and blood? Does a real son ever tell his mother not to come, especially when there's a precious new *einekel* on the scene?

Ouch. It really hurts. To be unwanted at such a milestone in my children's lives feels like a hornet plunging its stinger deeper and deeper into the fabric of my soul. *Now, Self, I counseled, you know you're being unreasonable. They just had a baby, and you don't want to be in the way. Thank Hashem that they're being honest! Would you have wanted to stay on if you weren't really wanted?* But then the other voice countered. *Me? In the way? Me? A hindrance? I would help; I would do whatever they wanted, from cooking to cleaning to holding that beautiful baby and anything in between.*

We're your parents, after all — yes, I am, too, Chaim. Don't you remember, my Chaim? I helped you with homework, took you to doctors, soothed your fears, listened to your concerns, bandaged your bruises, cheered you on at your sports games... I mothered you, Chaim. And how often do we see you? Don't you want to see us?

I davened for this *simchah* for so many years. While you waited for your arms to be filled, I poured my heart into your aching pain and murmured *perek* after *perek* of *Tehillim*, asking Hashem to deposit assorted, hard-earned mitzvos that I performed into your "account." And now, I've been rebuffed. That's the way it is; it's the new generation. In my day, no one asked me how long they could stay or if it was a convenient time when they planned a visit. My in-laws just gave us their itinerary, and I smiled and tried to be a good daughter-in-law, even when it was hard.

Chaim sent me some gorgeous pictures this morning, and my heart melted when I saw him holding his new son. What a *neis*, a beautiful, healthy baby. Chaim, my Chaim, a father.

I called on Sunday just to check in, see how the *shalom zachor* was and ask how they were doing.

"Where are you staying?" Shaindy asked, and I told her we'd be staying with my close friend.

"Oh, that's nice," she said, "and what are your plans in the end?"

When I explained that it didn't sound like the best time for us to hang around, so we'd just zip in and out, she agreed. "Yeah, sounds good. Maybe another time, Ima."

Yeah. Maybe…

If only Chaim had called and assured us that he would have loved for us to stay longer but Shaindy wasn't feeling well, perhaps the pain wouldn't be as raw. Any excuse would have made me feel better instead of feeling rejected.

I love you, Chaim and Shaindy. May you be *zocheh* to raise him *l'Torah l'chuppah ul'maasim tovim*.

My body feels so drained and utterly exhausted in a way I've never experienced before. Obsessed with the idea of sleeping, my brain can't even contemplate anything more complex than the following one-syllable words when the phone rings.

"Hi, Ima. You-want-to-come-stay-with-us-now. Oh-I-see-well-that's-nice-we'll-get-back-to-you-soon. Bye-have-a-nice-day."

I close my eyes once again and have just drifted off into blissful sleep when a newborn's crying pierced the hazy webs of confusion where, until three days ago, a sharp brain used to dwell.

Baby…whose baby is crying? After years of yearning, davening, and hoping, is this little one actually ours? Why, then, don't I feel anything except numbness? When I attempt to shake it off, anxiety seems to take its place, which feels even worse. How will I have the stamina to take care of this helpless little person when I lack the energy to walk from the bedroom to the kitchen? And why do I just feel like crying? A primal, inexplicable need for my mother to take care of me fills me with a sense of utter dependency.

Somewhere in the deep recesses of my mind, something seems wrong with this picture. Everyone else is smiling and crying from joy. I certainly already love this little person. But can Chaim just ask everyone to turn off the noise and call my mother?

"Your parents want to come for Shabbos? This Shabbos?"

"They want to help."

"Chaim, I like your parents very much and I don't want to hurt your mother. She's a very kind and sensitive woman. But I can't right now. I don't feel like myself physically or emotionally.

"I'm sure you'll find a way to explain to them, and they'll understand that a girl just needs her mother, especially after a first child. None of the childbirth classes prepared me for how sore and achy I feel all over. As comfortable as I am with your family, there's still a feeling of wanting to be at my best when they're around, and right now, I don't even feel like me. Your mother had so many children, I'm sure she understands my state of body and mind better than most people.

"Thanks, Chaim, for understanding, and can you please dim the lights on your way out so I can get some sleep? It's hard to imagine ever feeling alert and energetic again. Tell your mother to come another time. She really is such a wonderful lady."

12

SURPRISE PACKAGE

Rachel Speaks:

The big, brown, ubiquitous UPS truck rumbled to a stop right outside our modest ranch home. Within a moment, all my children and I converged from different sections of the house, gathering at the living room's bay window to see what was coming our way. We held our collective breath as the truck opened its cavernous mouth and an intrepid UPS veteran bore a bulky package aloft until he deposited it at our doorstep. With a jaunty wave, he was gone, and in a superb display of teamwork, we panted and lugged the big package into our kitchen.

"What could it be?" Yehudis asked.

"It's from Grandma," Rivkie announced, noticing the return address.

Armed with a kitchen scissors and steely determination, I broke through the layers of packing tape and opened the box. Thousands of white Styrofoam peanuts greeted my eyes, and I sighed as they spilled over my floor while I reached in to find what was under them. Finally, I saw it. A big, brown, archaic serving bowl, looking like it came right out of *Little House on the Prairie.* Just to give you an insider's glimpse, I detest shopping and would have to seriously debate, if given the choice, going to a medical appointment vs. spending a few hours in this oh-so-feminine pastime. My mother-in-law, however, firmly believes in shopping as a significant, house-wifely occupation, and fills her home and ours with the results of her obsession. Thankfully, we live in different cities. However, even I have some taste preferences, and this bowl was definitely not one of them.

"Hey, there's another one!" Yossi shouted, his arms completely submerged inside the peanuts. Triumphantly, he withdrew another cellophane-wrapped, colonial-style, two-handled brown bowl — only this one was in pieces. I sighed with relief. *At least I would only have to keep one such bowl.*

My husband called his mother later that evening. "Thank you for the present."

"Oh, I'm so glad you like it," she enthused. "Isn't it a great set?"

A firm believer in the value of honesty, my husband made his first blunder.

"It's very nice, but the piece with the handles was broken."

"Broken?" My mother-in-law was shocked and upset. "I wonder how that happened. I told them to wrap it well."

Up went the unbroken relic to take its honorable place on an attic shelf (to be taken down and used the next time Mom visited), while its broken mate went into the garbage. Naïvely, I assumed the story was over.

Several days later, the UPS truck was back. Warily, I watched our new friend (same guy; he gave us a smile this time) make the trek again from the back of his truck to our front door. For some reason, I wasn't surprised to see my in-laws' return address on the outside of the box, and my heart plummeted. Reaching inside the ubiquitous peanuts, I extracted the same two-handled bowl, only this time it was in even more pieces than the first one.

"So, do you love it?" Mom asked me as I rolled my eyes and cradled the receiver between neck and ear.

"Thank you," I replied evasively. "But this one came broken, too."

Mom was not to be deterred. UPS came by several more times over the next few weeks. Each time I saw the truck, my eyes began to water; I wasn't sure whether to laugh or cry, so I did a little of both.

Finally the day arrived. A package came, covered in even more peanuts and thicker layers of cellophane. Ever so carefully I reached inside and withdrew the earthenware serving bowl with large handles on either side; it was massive, it was brown, it was oval shaped, and it certainly wouldn't fit into any of my kitchen cabinets.

"You did it!" my husband told his mother.

"Hurray!" she crowed. "Just enjoy it."

I grabbed the bowl and heaved my way up the attic steps.

"There," I told it, "at least you have company," and I set it firmly beside its counterpart.

Several years passed, and every so often, our family was treated to a surprise package. A Seder plate whose designer must have received a prize for originality, a three-piece crockpot set that took up an entire counter, with each individual pot holding only one quart. *Well, considering we're fourteen people, that could feed about half of us at a time,* I mused, grateful to have attic storage. A big, beautiful silver coffee tureen that would keep your coffee warm for hours…just what I always wanted and needed, I'd just never realized.

Now how could I turn this saga into an article? I wondered, furrowing my brow and thinking hard. Could I inject depth into materialistic frenzy? Well, perhaps this experience could be a *mashal* for our lives in This World. After 120 years, we'll bring our carefully wrapped packages before the Melech Malchei HaMelachim, anxiously awaiting His reaction. Will we bring hopelessly outdated commodities that are cumbersome and unnecessary? Will HaKadosh Baruch Hu laugh at our puny purchases that we exerted so much effort to acquire in This World?

My most recent package arrived this past *erev Shabbos*. Uh-oh. I turned to my cleaning lady, and we exchanged grins. She's been with us for years so she's seen her share of packages.

"Here goes," I exclaimed, and she held her sides, laughing, watching, and waiting.

"One solid bamboo cutting board with a drip tray," I read, grunting as I placed the large, heavy board on my table. "Just what I always wanted."

And then came the box inside the box.

"A roasting rack." I stared at the metal rack, and it looked back at me wordlessly.

"Now what exactly do I do with this?" I turned to my cleaning lady, now doubled over, her entire body convulsed with laughter.

"I don't know, Rachel. But when you find out, you let me know," she gasped.

I erupted in sidesplitting laughter, enjoying the freedom to just laugh and enjoy life.

Thanks, Mom. That was just what I needed.

Eileen Speaks:

Good morning, Sol. Would you mind getting me a copy of the Sunday sales on your way back from shul? You know how I love to save money, and maybe I can find something for that hardworking daughter-in-law of mine. They live with the bare minimum, yet I love to decorate her home with lovely, stylish items."

"Now, Eileen, do you think they have anywhere left to put more decorations? Their seven kids do take up a lot of space."

I laughed, "Listen, Sol, trust me, a woman loves pretty things. Didn't our son, the rabbi, quote a Torah source saying that a man needs to buy something pretty for his wife every holiday?"

This argument was foolproof. He had to agree with me. Besides, this daughter-in-law is so complex, I never know if what I say pleases her or brings tears. When it comes to shopping, that is my area of expertise. I know that no woman can resist pretty gifts, and making her happy is also a way of giving to our son.

So, now that we have determined the facts on the table, I can't wait to see the sales! Did I say table? Hmmm… table! Magnificent salad bowls to grace their table. Maybe Rachel thinks that I didn't notice, but those disposable salad bowls from the dollar store have got to go. Ugh, how utterly tasteless! I'll very tactfully mention it to her in our next conversation. I wouldn't want their guests to think they lack class. What happens when prospective in-laws start asking about their table-setting habits? Rachel should know better, as her own sister is a matchmaker. I shudder to think of the potential consequences if she continues to use these bowls. Sol will be so proud of my extra sensitivity and how hard I work to be a mother, not just a mother-in-law, to Rachel. Okay, Eileen, off to your favorite pastime, destination — the mall! Objective: new salad bowls for Mitchell and Rachel.

Shopping is so exhilarating. Maybe I should invite her to join me and give her a chance to get out. She'd love it. So many pretty things to choose from. Let's see…huge salad bowls. That should feed their family. And such lovely, dainty crockpots for their *cholent*. I know some of their kids like potatoes and others don't, so this allows for differentiation. Eileen, you are one great Bubby, you even know the buzzwords in education today. I wonder why more people don't call for child-rearing advice.

It's not easy to be a long-distance grandmother, but modeling generosity can't hurt for now or even when I'm no longer here so they can remember me fondly.

Hmmm… So many salad bowls to choose from, but no need to worry about price when it comes to those darling children. Just beauty, good quality, and usefulness. And some of the more overweight children could use a bit more salad and a bit less other stuff. I must advise Rachel about nutrition tips for her kids. It's hard to imagine what she'd do without my help and advice.

"Ma'am, could you please wrap this well to ensure there is no breakage? These bowls have a very special purpose and need to be shipped quite some distance. I expect that the store will take full responsibility for these items to arrive safely?"

You know, I used to feel a bit ashamed of my penchant for shopping. It does seem a bit frivolous on the surface. But now that I've matured, I recognize that there are limitless opportunities to give to my children. This week salad bowls and next week, a varied *cholent* set. The possibilities are endless.

"Sol, do you think Rachel even knows how lucky she is? Maybe I should let her know in our next conversation. Don't worry, Sol, I'll say it tactfully, always tactfully."

I knew they'd get the gift within a week. I didn't wait for them to call; I was too excited to hear Rachel's reaction. "So, kids, how are you enjoying the stunning, new salad bowls? Bet you never saw anything like them before, right? Did you say they came broken?! Why, that is absolutely unforgivable. I'm going straight back to the mall to have them reship a brand-new set. I don't have to, you say? No, I won't have it any other way. When it comes to you kids, nothing is too difficult.

"Rachel, you know, in life we have to be assertive to make things happen. Just wait till I say my piece to the manager. No children of mine will ever receive broken shards again."

13

TENTACLES OF FEAR

Sarah Speaks:

Tentacles of fear and sadness gripped my heart as I watched my beloved father-in-law struggle to get up from his chair and perform other everyday functions, like eating, reaching, and following a conversation. It seemed clear that his physical weakness stemmed from the cruel dementia that had taken up residence in his once fertile and rich mind. You could almost see, perhaps from the vacant look in his eyes, that his brain was refusing to send signals to his body, and therefore his limbs refused to perform.

I've always cherished our special relationship, and seeing his deterioration is excruciatingly painful. Having grown up without a father, my heart swelled every time he told me I'm like a daughter to him. I'd always respond that he was like a father to me.

How can a brilliant, philosophical, successful doctor become a shadow of himself? *Dad*, I sometimes want to shout, *you can beat this! Don't let it get you, you're too good, too smart, too everything.* And then the tears come.

Mom (my mother-in-law) gives me periodic updates by phone, telling me he can't button his shirts or knot his tie, he needs help getting dressed, or he says something nonsensical. My heart clenches with a physical pain as I listen, and sometimes she cries.

"He was so smart, Sarah," she says. "It seems like this disease always picks the smartest ones."

I mull that one over. *Exactly how high does one's IQ have to be to qualify*, I wonder, while at the same time reminding myself that everything is *b'yad Hashem*.

"Mom is overwhelmed," I told my husband. "It's really too much for a ninety-year-old woman to be a 24/7 nurse. Dad needs help at night, too. Can't we do something?" The assisted living home where they live only offers help in an emergency, but a person has to be independent in caring for his own daily needs.

But they weren't ready for our help. Mom insisted on caring for Dad, even though she often complained that it was too hard for her. So I listened, empathized, and felt frustrated and helpless against the tide of an increasingly debilitating situation. Then one day everything changed.

"Mark," Mom had said to Dad, startled. "Why are you babbling? And what's wrong with your shoulder? Why is one side higher than the other?"

A nurse called an ambulance, and Dad was rushed to the hospital. After several days of testing, the reports came back that he hadn't suffered a stroke, and they weren't sure what had caused his sudden deterioration. He was sent to rehab for several weeks. And then came the crash. Dad was no longer eligible to live with Mom. He no longer met the criteria for their memory care unit and had to live elsewhere.

When I called him in his new residence, my heart broke into a thousand pieces as I heard his familiar deep tenor. He told me, "I miss my wife. I don't understand why I can't be with her."

"I'm sorry, Dad," I empathized, fighting back a tidal wave of emotion. "That's really rough. But she comes every day, right?" I knew she had been there the day before.

"No," he answered emphatically. "I can't remember the last time I saw her."

I called Mom to check in and absorbed the volumes of her pain.

"Going down to meals without him is so painful, Sarah," she cried. "I miss him so much, and all the other couples sit together… except…"

"This isn't a viable solution," I told my husband. "We've got to get him back with her somehow. It's just so wrong. How do you separate a husband and wife?"

My idea of hiring help was rejected — too costly — so I racked my brains for an idea. I sent Mom an email:

> Dear Mom,
> Since Dad is walking now, do you think your facility would reevaluate his condition and perhaps allow him to move back with you? I'm happy to call them and arrange for the evaluation.

The response came shortly.

> Sarah,
> I feel bad that you think I'm not capable of getting him

reevaluated. I took care of all his needs, handle all the bills, and take the bus to see him every day…besides, he can't come back here, as hiring 24/7 help is too expensive. That's why I just moved to a small suite, to save money.

Oh no. I realized she'd taken my message the wrong way, and that I'd better respond quickly. The dynamics of a mother-in-law/daughter-in-law relationship never fail to amaze me. You can have the best of intentions, say and do everything right, but your motives can still be suspect.

Mom Speaks:

Tentacles of fear gripped my heart as the nurses took away my life partner. They murmured some platitudes that didn't even penetrate about how the new place is so much better able to provide for all of his needs, and of course I could visit him daily. What do they understand about separating a wife from her husband of over fifty years? Visitations? Is this the end of our dreams of caring for each other throughout old age?

Oh, the relentless guilt. Its cumbersome waves wash over me as my inner critic loudly berates me for worrying about my own loneliness. *What about your husband, who was once so smart, capable, and a support system to the entire family? Why are you just selfishly thinking about yourself?* He must be petrified and confused as he slips in and out of lucid moments, wondering why his wife abandoned him when he needs her most.

At least my own brain seems to function. I take comfort in my independence and ability to take care of the finances, meal planning, and all of our medical needs. It is vitally important to me to put on a tough front for my children. If they ever suspected my limitations and vulnerabilities, maybe I'd also have to live out my years with patients suffering from mental deterioration. No matter what, I will maintain an upper lip in front of my kids. *Be strong, honey, be strong.*

As a young child, old age always scared me. My sister loved to visit old age homes, but I couldn't handle seeing the once vibrant people who'd become shadows of their prior selves, with hardly the energy to stand on their own two feet. I remember going with my class in eighth grade to a nursing home and seeing an old lady screaming from a wheelchair. It looked like she was staring at me, yet when I got closer, she wasn't focused on me at all, just screaming strings of words. I ran back shaking to the school bus and waited for the other students to return. Now, my own husband is living in that same kind of institution, and I am terrified it could happen to me.

Judging from the email conversation between my daughter-in-law and me today, I'm worried that my children are already doubting I have what it takes to cope anymore. Imagine Sarah offering to arrange for *my husband* to be reevaluated. After everything I've done and continue to do, they think I'm losing it. I'm not losing it!

14

YIKES! MOM'S MOVING IN!

Shulamis Speaks:

Shaking my head, I wondered if I'd heard correctly. Did Asher just ask me if I would be open to his mother moving in with us? He's not serious, is he? But one look at his expression assured me he was quite serious and anxiously awaiting my response.

"Asher, I'd love to be a *tzadeikes* and say yes, but you know how rocky my relationship with Mom has always been, growing more so as she ages. I'm concerned that I'm not up to the challenge."

Asher was quiet and just looked at me steadily.

"I know, I know what you're thinking. After all we owe our parents, how dare I even consider saying no? But isn't my mental sanity worth something?"

Asher exhaled loudly. "Just think about it," he said, and with great reluctance, I agreed.

Mom moving in; what would that do to my life? Well, for one, I'd probably be late to almost every place I tried to go. Dad used to joke that Mom had two speeds: slow and very slow. She tends to remember things precisely at the time we're supposed to leave. The second problem is her incessant talking. I'm an introvert, at least partially so, and I thrive on introspection and periods of silence. If she talked to me all day, I don't know how I'd stand it.

Mom also tends to be very critical, especially if there's an overweight child in the house or if anyone doesn't do something appropriate for his or her physical health. "It doesn't hurt to be good-looking," is the credo she spouts at frequent intervals, and Hashem should save the one who doesn't aspire to look their very best while in my mother-in-law's presence. I have one child who's overweight, and whenever she sees him enjoying food he "shouldn't" have, he's in dire straits. Mom shows her concern and love by grabbing food out of his hands, explaining the risks of being overweight while tears gather in his eyes.

"Do you want to have a heart attack or get diabetes?" she demands.

I have another child who's not the greatest tooth brusher and needs reminders. The last time Mom visited, she gave this child an hour-long lecture on tooth brushing, how her teeth should look as white as a sheet, how disappointed she is…

Basically, the mental health of my entire family is at stake if we go ahead with this insane plan.

I think we should find a good assisted living facility in our vicinity, and we'll visit frequently. But as I imagine proposing this option to Asher, I feel pangs of guilt stab my heart. After all, she's his mother and my mother-in-law, which equals obligation. So many people make this sacrifice with love and devotion. I don't know how they find the inner strength; maybe I'm a *rasha*? Should I say yes?

Asher Speaks:

It's hard to believe that I, Mr. Practical, Mr. Cerebral, Mr. Logical (and the rest of the nicknames that typify my lack of emotionalism), feel literally torn apart by the recent role reversal in my life. My opinionated, strong mother has suddenly become so vulnerable, terrified to be on her own, insecure in decision-making, and very needy. My heart muscles that successfully avoided working out for years are being challenged to face this reality without tears and pain — and failing miserably at this task.

My wife, who for years has begged me not to fix but just to listen and validate, doesn't recognize her new, teary, reflective husband worrying about his lonely mother. And it probably doesn't help our relationship that she sees my mother as the main beneficiary of this newly discovered tenderness, particularly as their connection has been strained to its limits throughout our marriage.

My mother communicates directly (some may even call it blunt), yet to me, this is just Mom talking. She has strong opinions about everything, ranging from appearance, style, household decoration, and child-rearing, and loves to share them with my wife. My wife's middle name is sensitive and not unexpectedly takes great offense at my mother's perceived interference and lack of tact, particularly when it appears to be directly targeting one of our children.

I give my wife a lot of credit for her efforts over the years in hosting and welcoming my mother despite the anguish she suffers before, during, and after every visit. Have I ever told her, you ask? No, the old me may not have even noticed, much less mentioned a word. More food for reflection.

Over the years, I watched from afar as a number of my slightly older peers took in their elderly parents and cared for their needs. I admired the sacrifice and thought of the great example they were setting for their children, not unaware of the challenges of having three generations live harmoniously under one roof. I picture kids running around, eating at all hours of the day, the elderly parents craving peace and quiet, and the sandwich generation doing their best to cater to all needs while neglecting their own.

Ambivalence, what a tortuous state. Part of me wants to take in my mother and care for her. I love her. She gave birth to me and raised me. Yet, another part of me sees the storm I would be letting loose in my own home. How can I even ask this of my wife? Yes, I know she's kind and runs a volunteer organization for elderly people almost singlehandedly. But her home is her refuge. She writes actively and finally reached a relatively peaceful time as many of our children have moved out of the house. She needs her space, and my mother doesn't know the meaning of the word. Yet, what of my sacred obligation to honor my mother? Can I leave her in her helplessness and not fulfill the role Hashem seems to be placing on my shoulders? Is this the example I want to set for my children? Part of me almost wishes for my wife to refuse; then I can get rid of this awful guilt because I can tell myself that I tried. How many fragments can one heart hold?

Well, my wife has been asking for communication for years. I somehow don't think this is exactly what she envisioned, but I think the time has come for me to share my sentiments and even ask her if just maybe she could find it in her heart to invite my mother to live with us. I know it will be hard, but maybe with her new, more understanding husband, we can navigate this together.

"Um, honey, can we talk?"

15

SHATTERED DREAMS

Aviva Speaks:

Young and idealistic, I dreamed of marrying and supporting a *talmid chacham* who would learn as long as possible. What better foundation for my *bayis ne'eman* than the *kedushah* of Torah? I would work with love, becoming a partner in eternity as my husband toiled day and night. A picture of bliss I held close to my heart.

Music played, Avrami stomped on the glass, and with resounding mazal tovs and ecstatic dancing, my dream began to play out. We settled into our apartment, and I landed a job as a nurse in a local hospital soon after, thanking Hashem for helping me begin to lay our foundation. But the hours were long, the work intense, and somehow, in addition to my twelve-hour shifts, I had to muster the strength to take care of the house, prepare dinners and Shabbosim — served with a smile, please! And then our precious baby entered the scene. I was in a perpetual whirlwind of tension and overwhelmed as I raced from work to the babysitter, trying to pacify the baby and put up dinner at the same time. Often, when the baby's cries escalated, my tears joined his and we cried together.

Yet when Avrami came home, I pulled myself together, put a warm smile on my face, and made sure that he never fathomed my internal upheaval. I was managing fine, thank you, and it was my pleasure and privilege to support this holy endeavor. Yet, if this was so heavenly and sublime, why did I feel like I was slowly unraveling, piece by piece?

By the time baby number two announced her arrival, dinner had become a hurried and simple affair, the house was in perpetual shambles, and I felt like I was constantly panting my way up a steep precipice, yet never reaching the longed-for peak. I had no social life (who had the time or energy?) and I was tired. So very tired.

"Avrami," I timidly ventured, shuddering as I dipped my toes into frigid waters, "I think I need to cut back on my hours. I'm just not managing. And I wondered, I mean, would it be possible for you to stay home for night *seder*?"

The complete look of shock on Avrami's face made me want to tuck my head and toes into a shell and never come out. His expression showed disillusionment, betrayal, and pain, the loss of a dream. *How could I do this to him*, his eyes cried, *after a mere two years of kollel?* We had talked long-term, anywhere from ten to twenty years. I had promised. And now, just when he was swimming the length and breadth of the Talmudic ocean, just when he was starting to achieve his goals and make real progress, I was snatching the prize from him and forcing him to be content with less.

What kind of wimp was I, anyway? I wondered. And why did it seem like the rest of the *kollel* wives worldwide managed their loads with ease and dignity while I struggled under my miniscule burden? How could I do this to him? Would I be able to live with myself knowing I wasn't living up to the commitment I made? Maybe I should keep pushing myself and ignore my feelings. After all, a promise is a promise.

"Maybe you're just having a hard day," Avrami finally said in response to my query. "The baby's been teething…"

When he said those words, I realized that I could continue pretending, but somewhere along the line it would backfire. He wouldn't have the same wife he married, but rather a robotic shadow performing the motions. And that's when the dam broke and the floodgates were unleashed.

"No," I sobbed, "it's not just a day or two or even a week. I haven't managed since Yossi was born, and now that Chanale's here, my life feels like a nightmare. I'm sorry, Avrami, I really am. I wanted this to work so badly. I was totally committed to this ideal. But," I choked in a whisper, "I can't do this anymore. I'm really sorry."

Avrami Speaks:

So many people focus on the challenges facing girls in today's *shidduch* market. Yet as a recently married guy, I know firsthand that we, too, have many difficulties in this area. Just the sheer volume of dating suggestions for me overwhelmed my mother. At the same time she was wringing her hands anxiously, waiting for the phone to ring with some reasonable suggestions for my sister. And then there was the task of attempting to find a respectful way to narrow down the list and figure out which girls were most compatible. Marathon talks with my *rebbeim*, trying to ensure that I was being genuine with my aspirations and that my goals were grounded and reality based. Finally, we chose a girl who grew up in a family with rock solid Torah values and who wanted nothing more than for her husband to learn Torah as long as possible. She longed for a home where Torah permeated the very air and transformed her family. It sounded like a match made on Sinai.

Usually, my first dates were rather neutral. With Aviva, there was a palpable excitement in the air as we practically anticipated each other's opinions and enjoyed the time together as the minutes flew by. After four dates, we dropped the *shadchan*, knowing it was just a matter of time before we became an officially engaged couple. Smooth was not the word; our *shadchan* must have been delighted at the seamless transition from "if" to "when," and from "I" to "we."

Aviva and I discussed the expected topics of goals and where we each saw ourselves in five years and ten years, smiling knowingly as our dreams coincided. It was as though we had rehearsed a pre-arranged script. Our parents were thrilled. Now my mother could give her full concentration to marrying off my sister. My *kallah's* family was ecstatic. Why not? They had just gotten the "best boy in the yeshivah," all modesty aside. And I felt so grateful to have such a wonderful *kallah*. We dreamed together of setting up my friends with her friends and ending the *shidduch* crisis tomorrow.

Married life with Aviva was even better than I envisioned. I maintained my rigorous study schedule and she took obvious pride in my achievements. The qualitative difference it made to my learning to have a personal coach encouraging me propelled me forward in ways that even caused my *chavrusos* to marvel. Wellsprings of new understandings just seemed to bubble out from the recesses of my mind. I thanked Hashem every day for the ideal life partner that He granted me, who wanted nothing more than for her husband to become a Torah scholar.

Recently, though, something felt different in the atmosphere when I came home at night. Although Aviva continued to greet me with a smile, there was an unfamiliar strained look peeking out from underneath the smile, almost as if the smile felt forced. When I asked her if everything was okay, she reverted quickly to sharing the antics of our *kinderlach* and the interesting events at work in her normal, bubbly way, and I attributed the earlier furrow to the women's moods I'd learned about in my wedding preparation classes.

Later that week, the bubble burst. My dear wife, Aviva, spilled out her heart. She was completely overwhelmed, and the reality of her responsibilities far exceeded anything she'd pictured during our dating process. Tears cascaded down her face and I felt terrible knowing she'd been suffering, yet I still felt that the rug was being pulled out from under me. Were my dreams about to evaporate like a puff of smoke?

Our first long talk definitely wouldn't be endorsed by leading marriage experts. We were both talking and focused on our own pain and neither of us was listening. I told her I'd speak to my *rebbeim* and we'd find a solution together. Then I escaped to my yeshivah, away from the guilt-provoking intensity of her tears. Much to my surprise, my own tears poured forth as I told my *rebbi* about the recent events. I had at least ten years of Torah study goals. I lived and breathed for the atmosphere and wrestling in learning. Furthermore, what happened to our shared dream?

Every time I resolved to be more sympathetic to my wife, my visions of a nine-to-five job and giving up my aspirations disrupted my good intentions. Aviva apologized and life continued as normal.

I helped out more and hoped it was just a passing phase. For the next six months, Aviva and I talked about everything except for this unspoken topic, which was foremost on both of our minds. However, I could no longer ignore Aviva's obvious exhaustion or the long shadows under her eyes.

My *rebbi* patiently helped me understand my obligations toward my wife. It's not her responsibility to take care of the family and provide financial support. And, yes, she did want to, but life's reality challenged that.

At the end of the day, do I want my dreams fulfilled if they've become my wife's nightmares and they come at the expense of her physical and emotional health? Aviva told me she feels terrible, she deeply wanted me to pursue my Torah studies with true sincerity, but that she just can't manage and her strength is waning.

I can choose to be resentful and play the blame game, or I can choose to accept this as direction from Hashem. Maybe Hashem wants a different type of service plan than the one I envisioned. I can continue my love of Torah and make it a priority every day. Aviva and I both want that. But I can also take the financial pressure off my wife by contributing to the family finances. It will be difficult particularly as I pass my yeshivah and yearn to be fully immersed. Yet I am certain I won't lose out in any way by being the husband and father that Hashem wants me to become. It's time for me to comfort Aviva who has been tormenting herself.

"Aviva, what do you think about me enrolling in this Agudah-sponsored accounting course? And, Aviva, I want you to have an early night tonight while I learn at home. You need some rest."

16

OH LOOK!

Batya Speaks:

Oh look, a letter from South Africa! I wonder how Shmuly and Chavie are enjoying the beautiful summer weather; we have three feet of snow covering the ground. Every time we get a letter, it reminds me of my seventh date with Yanky. Hard to believe it's been twenty years already...

"So tell me more about what it was really like growing up in South Africa. It must have been such a culture shock traveling overseas to yeshivah and leaving your family so far away."

"I will admit to being homesick, and the guys good-naturedly *imitated my accent all the time. But you'll love my family and they really want to meet you. Am I getting ahead of myself over here, Batya?"*

It was the first time he called me by my name.

The next date, he proposed and we were officially chasan and kallah. And, oh, the excitement that began to fill my heart; this was really happening.

Having grown up in a very small family, I longed for the sense of belonging to a larger whole. If Yanky's family was anything like him, I could look forward to a whole new family ready to welcome me with open arms. Thank You, Hashem, for such a *chasan* and for realizing my dream of a large, dynamic family to share.

Yet life has a way of leading us in unexpected directions. Five years after our marriage, we received a magnificent invitation to my brother-in-law's bar mitzvah.

"Yanky, can you believe your brother is making a bar mitzvah next month? I'm so excited to go to South Africa and see the family again. It's been quite a while."

"Um, Batya…"

"Yanky, this is so exciting! I need to shop! Do you think I should wear my black dress or get a new dress for the occasion?"

"Batya…

"Yes, Yanky? Oh, and I definitely need new shoes, and you need a suit. We need to give your family *nachas*."

"Batya, there's something I need to discuss with you."

"Oh, sure, Yanky, any time, always happy to hear what you have to say. Why don't we first just finish this South Africa shopping list and then I'll be all ears."

"Batya, what I need to discuss pertains directly to South Africa."

"Oh, Yanky, why didn't you say so? Don't tell me your brother sent extra funding to handle these expenses! You know, maybe that's just too much for us to accept."

OH LOOK! **103**

"Batya, I really need to talk with you right now."

"Oh, Yanky, I enjoy our talks too. Can you believe it's been five years since we were there? Can I make you a coffee?"

"Batya, this is very hard for me to explain. I know you want to go back to South Africa and see the family. But my brother's funding is a bit dry at the moment — I'm sorry, Batya, he only sent one ticket, a ticket for me."

My jaw dropped open. Trying to conceal the pain, disappointment, and even the sense of betrayal that my husband would willingly go without me, I swallowed the growing lump in my throat.

"Oh, well I guess I'll just toss this list then. You go, have a great time, and give everyone my best. Tickets are expensive. I understand."

This pattern repeated itself every couple of years for varied *simchahs*. A single ticket would arrive in the mail, and Yanky would fly away to that magnificent country to enjoy quality time with his family while I stayed home nursing disappointment and trying to cleanse myself from the hurt. Aren't I part of the family too?

Why do they just want Yanky?

Yet, always wanting to be the good wife, I summoned a tremulous smile and packed him off with lots of food and warm wishes to enjoy while the kids and I counted the days till his return.

Fast-forward twenty years. My brother-in-law was preparing a huge bash in South Africa for my in-laws' fiftieth anniversary. Mentally preparing myself for that familiar feeling of self-pity and exclusion, plus a gold star award for martyrdom, I opened the familiar South African-stamped letter.

> Dear Yanky and Batya,
>
> Enclosed are two tickets for you and Batya to join us at the upcoming anniversary party. Can't wait to see you there.
>
> Love,
> Your brother Shmuly

"Yanky, Yanky, can we talk?"

"Batya, haven't we had these talks for so many years? I thought you understand my need to see my family and our own limited budget."

"Yanky!

"Yes, Batya, I know it's hard for you. I wish it could be different."

"Yanky, please listen!"

"Batya, I can repeat each of our parts in this conversation in my sleep. Maybe we should take each other's lines for some variety."

I stuck the letter under his nose and pulled out the two tickets with shining eyes.

"I guess this means we're official now. Which dress should I wear to the anniversary party?"

Shmuly Speaks:

"Chavy, we need to talk about the bar mitzvah." I turned to my wife with a smile, excited to plan our first real *simchah* together.

"I know. I can't believe it's coming up so soon. Just three more months and so much to do! I have to outfit all the kids, talk to the caterer and the band…"

"Yep, all those things need to be taken care of. No one said making a *simchah* is easy. But I was thinking about something else. Do you know it's been five years since I last saw my brother? I'd really like to send Yanky a ticket. He's my only brother and he should be with us for a family *simchah*."

"That's really generous of you, Shmuly. Especially now when things are a little tight."

"Well, I know he can't afford to come unless we bring him in. I wish we could send one for Batya, too, but I just don't see how we can. Between all the expenses that keep cropping up, two tickets would put us over the top. But I think we can handle one."

"So do it!" Chavy said. "It will be so nice for the two of you to have some time together. I'm sure Batya will understand."

A few years and another mazal tov later…
"Mazal tov, mazal tov!" Chavy beamed as she called family and friends with the amazing news. Shoshi was a *kallah*!

A few nights later, once the initial excitement had ebbed a bit, my wife and I sat on the couch talking over cups of hot tea.

"You know, Chavy, here we go again. This is feeling like *déjà vu*. I really want to send Yanky a ticket for the wedding. Do we have the extra money? Not really. We have this five-year commitment to supporting the kids in *kollel*, plus all the wedding expenses. Invitations, gowns, suits, hall, caterer, *sheitels*, kitchen stuff and linens… is there an end? Our business is doing okay, baruch Hashem, but there's a limit. I think we have to cut where we can. So I guess I'll send one ticket again. I wish we could bring them both in, but…"

"You can only do what you can do," Chavy murmured, sipping her tea. "We're not made of money, you know. And we are making a wedding. They'll just have to understand."

I hoped they really did understand. I wondered how I would feel if the tables were turned. Was Batya really okay with this situation, or were there unknown blisters festering? Shaking my head, I decided not to dwell on it. It's not like we could change the situation anyway.

With each *simchah* the same scenario replayed.

Fast-forward twenty years…
"We should really do something for Ma and Ta's 50th. What

do you think?" As I turned to my wife and life partner, I knew she would be happy to create a memorable celebration for our parents.

"You're right, Shmuly. Such a special occasion calls for something big," Chavy agreed.

"You know, I've been thinking. Our kids are all married, and our years of support are long over. Plus, Hashem sent me a special gift this month. We just picked up two new clients, and they're big ones. So this time, I think we can afford to bring in Yanky and Batya together. Won't that be nice?"

Chavy breathed a sigh of relief. If there really had been hard feelings over the years, maybe this would help them dissipate.

"Now that will be a real celebration. The whole family together!"

PART II

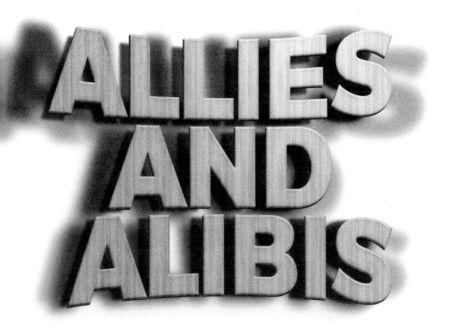

17

FIRED!

Zahava Speaks:

Straightening my shoulders, I smooth my *sheitel* as I walk toward the administrator's office. *It's just a meeting about next year, nothing to get all worked up about. They'll mention how much I've added to the office ambience, how much the patients appreciate my warm, personal touch, and hey, maybe they'll even offer me a raise. And I'll smile modestly, inwardly agreeing that I, young though I may be, surely am more computer savvy than all of them combined.*

"We don't know how we managed before you came on board, Zahava," the administrator will tell me, shaking her head with an *admiring smile on her lips. "So we'd like to invite you…"*

The only question is whether I should accept their offer of a contract renewal, or if I should be straight with them. I enjoy the challenge of working in this happening office. Dr. Hirsch is a renowned dermatologist, and people wait months to get an appointment with him. However, there's a long commute that's difficult to handle, especially now that I have to factor in the baby. So if I'd agree to stay on, it would have to be with the stipulation of an increase in salary.

I knock on Director Chaya Feinstein's door. She calls, "Come in," and I enter her office.

"Make yourself comfortable," she says, and I slide into a seat on the other side of her desk. "Thank you for coming," she greets me, in a business-like tone, folding her hands neatly on top of her cluttered desk.

Hmm, wonder what's eating her. She's usually so warm and friendly.

"Of course," I reply tersely. "Just to let you know, I really enjoy working here and love the interaction with patients. Hopefully, I've contributed also." I incline my head modestly before continuing. "Lately I've been busy updating our files and have switched to a more efficient communication mode."

Okay, Chaya, now it's time to make me an offer I can't refuse. To show how much you appreciate my dedication, my willingness to stay late, or to fill in for someone last minute…

She hesitates. "I don't know how to say this, Zahava. This is hard for me, too. Your work is excellent, and we really enjoy having you on staff. But due to some recent cutbacks, we're being forced to downsize. And sadly, the only logical place to start is with staff that has come on board more recently, irrespective of their stellar performance."

Huh? Didn't she read the script? Why do I feel like the rug was just pulled out from under me? I'm sinking. I will absolutely not cry in front of her. No way! But I do think I've been…fired!

"So I thank you for your wonderful year of service, but we won't be renewing your contract. I trust you'll find something well suited to your multifaceted talents."

"I understand," I say, nodding and pasting a thin smile on my lips while my insides implode in strident protest. "I wish you all the best."

I walk out standing tall, grateful they don't have X-ray vision to see my inner turmoil. *I've just been fired! Those total and complete incompetent fools just fired me!* Me, Zahava Green, *graduate of the Soroh Gold computer technology course. Of all the nerve! How dare they! Are they nuts? Don't they know I was head and shoulders above my classmates? How will they ever get the work done without me? That's the thanks I get for putting in overtime without a word of protest?!*

Granted, I was debating about resigning anyway. But that would have been okay; it would have been my decision, and I'd have felt so validated when they fell to their knees and begged me to stay on. But whoa, it hurts to be rejected. Being fired feels like part of my essence has been trampled. I know it's really for the good; I know I'll find something better. But my self-esteem has suffered a blow, and for now, it really hurts. Fired? Me?

I don't know if many people dream of becoming a human resource director. If we took polls of elementary school-aged children, there would be many more aspiring rabbis, firemen, nurses, and teachers. Yet I always was a nonconformist. Growing up in a very poor home and watching a widowed mother struggle to support her children, the seed of yearning to help people find jobs found a home in my heart. *What a joyful profession*, I daydreamed, *to pair the ideal candidate with the job best suited to his or her talents and abilities. What could be more satisfying than helping someone earn a respectable living and feeling the satisfaction of being productive?*

Focused on this lofty mission from the age of twelve, I took extra courses while still in high school and asked as many adults as possible how they found their jobs. I even dared to ask if they felt happy doing what they were doing for so many of their waking hours. Much to my idealistic distress, many said no, that they lived for vacation. I was horrified and determined to change the world. People spend years of their lives at work. I, Chaya, couldn't sit back and allow this dismal state of affairs to continue. Even as a student, my friends and I could identify the teachers who felt a passion for transmitting knowledge as opposed to those who appeared to just be doing a job. And those classes dragged by very slowly. Usually there were far more discipline issues as well. Did I behave, you wonder? Well, some things must remain confidential.

Fast-forward to my current position. I love the satisfaction of matching people to their ideal jobs. I love the sparkle of excitement when people learn that they've been hired for the position of their dreams. However, there is one aspect of my position I wish I could delete from my job description. When a company needs to downsize and the time comes to tell an employee that for various reasons her job will be terminated, there is no easy way to perform this surgery. Just knowing that the employee will experience rejection and betrayal, and that I'm the source of it, becomes my worst nightmare.

Often, an employee enters my office dreaming of receiving raises and accolades for a job well done, only to hear that the contract won't be renewed.

Just recently, I had to fire an employee by the name of Zahava Green. She walked confidently into my office with every reason to feel proud of her achievements. However, in the current economic climate, our business has the opportunity to save a significant amount of money by downsizing the number of staff members. Zahava truly deserves a raise, not to mention a transportation allowance for her commute. Yet I sense a growing dissatisfaction in her, as her intelligence far exceeds the nature of the work we can offer her.

I know Zahava, with her advanced skill set, will probably find something more suited to her talents and capabilities. Our decision makes sense on many levels, and yet it seems so unfair to cause pain to an employee who truly fulfilled every requirement of her job description and even made improvements in the efficiency of the office. At the same time, she is the newest employee, and we do have to show loyalty to our long-term employees. No one ever warned me about the hurtful aspect of human resource services.

Zahava is a truly talented and remarkable young woman. She doesn't belong here; she is capable of so much more. I know the time will come when she will thank me. Sometimes people remain in a safe environment, not venturing beyond because of fear of the unknown. I gave her a push, which may hurt in the moment but will likely become a source of momentum as she seeks to utilize her unique skills and earns a salary more commensurate with her education. If she only knew that underneath my confident and firm exterior her shock and dismay touch me deeply and make me question my own fit for this position.

Maybe I can write her a note expressing my willingness to write a warm letter of recommendation. In fact, I'll do that right now.

Dear Zahava,

It would be my pleasure to write you a note of recommendation. Please let me know if this will be helpful. Thank you for your wonderful service. We will miss having you here.

18

A LITTLE "CELL"F REFLECTION

Libby Speaks:

Just look around; no one talks to anyone else anymore. Bent over their devices, everyone is engrossed in their own worlds, which, in our technologically advanced society, doesn't even cause concern anymore. Back when I was growing up, carrying on a one-sided conversation could result in knowing glances followed by an urgent summons to the men in white coats.

I believe in personal communication, and unlike this modern decadent society, I model cell phone etiquette at its best. For example, my gym had to come up with a policy forbidding cell phones during class. Can you believe that was necessary? In the middle of aerobics and weight training, countless participants think nothing of walking off to schmooze on their phones, much to the teacher's incredulity and raised eyebrows (does raising eyebrows burn more calories? Maybe I'll try it). And how about in stores, when customers don't wish the cashier a good day because they're otherwise occupied in seemingly more significant conversations. Okay, time to get off my soapbox.

Oh, my cell phone is ringing. I'd better check to see if it's important. It's my only sister calling all the way from Eretz Yisrael! Because of the time difference, we often have trouble reaching each other.

"Hi, Shaindy, how are you? Baruch Hashem, just walking into a store, so don't mind if I try to keep my voice on the low end. You have something important to tell me? Okay, I'm all ears. Dovid is getting engaged tonight? Mazal tov! My nephew, wow! I want to hear all the details… Tell me everything. That's amazing, I'm so happy for you! Mazal tov!"

As we talked, I became aware of a hurt expression on the face of a dear friend who walked by me with her shopping cart. I nodded at her as she passed, but I was deeply engrossed in my sister's news. Surely she wasn't annoyed with me! I was finally talking with my only sister, and this was vitally important. If she knew the background, she would understand.

I continued listening to everything about this paragon of a *kallah* from the time she was in preschool.

Just as I was enjoying this detailed rendition, this friend walked by me once again and shook her head sadly and walked away. Now my conscience was activated. Did I unwittingly hurt her?

I said goodbye to Shaindy, now hyper-focused on the sad expression on my friend's face and feeling very guilty. Sometimes, no matter what we do, guilt has a way of worming its way into our heads and making itself feel quite at home. Should I not have given Shaindy my full attention? Should I have promised to call her back in order to greet my friend? Should I have explained to my friend about the nature of the chat even though they weren't official yet? No, that's a no-brainer. It was confidential and not my information to share.

Oh, well, more dilemmas to ponder, which will hopefully just allow me to grow.

The Cashier Speaks:

What a long journey from teaching in a classroom to working as a cashier. Logically, I understand that we moved late in the summer and the teaching jobs were taken already. Yet my heart feels so disappointed. What a difference when there's a passion and purpose in your work and lives can be transformed by a special relationship. I guess working as a cashier can help me become more humble. When someone I recognize observes me doing this job, I feel like crawling into a shell and hiding, unlike my experience as a teacher. Knowing I was a link in transmitting Torah to the next generation filled me with pride and self-respect. I stood up straight even during the most challenging of times. That thought deserves more reflection, as our jobs don't define us or determine our worth. But once again, that's logic speaking, which is a long distance away from my emotional reality.

But this time belongs to Tasty Tidbits. Maybe some solution-focused therapeutic strategies I used to implement in my classroom can help me here and now. Okay, let's give it a whirl. Self, are you listening? Since this is my current situation, I should try to accept and make the best of it. No matter the environment, I can help people, perhaps even transform lives. The power of a smile or kind word is awesome. And who knows? Maybe I can form new relationships with my coworkers and customers.

Here comes from my first opportunity. A customer is making her way toward my register right now.

Cashier: Good morning. I hope you found everything you needed.

Customer: Plastic bags, those large ziplock bags work really well.

Cashier: I'm glad you found them helpful.

Customer: Yes, my *sheitel* traveled without getting messed up at all and I saved schlepping that bulky box.

Cashier: Sorry, were you looking for a certain size bag? Aisle 4 has all of our bags of many assorted sizes.

Customer: You're so right. It is absolutely inspirational. I can't wait to tell people about this!

Cashier: Thank you. No one has ever been so gracious just to receive a bit of guidance.

Customer: Yes, awesome! Kiwis and pineapples would add a very colorful and healthy touch. Do you think you can help with that?

Cashier: My pleasure, the fruit is in aisle 2 and we got a beautiful shipment of kiwis in just today.

Customer: Absolutely. You know, you're incredibly helpful.

Cashier: Thank you, that's so nice of you to say. This is a new job and I'm so pleased to be able to help you.

Customer: One second, Chaya. Oh, excuse me, were you speaking to me? I'm on the phone with a very close friend. Just please add up my purchases and let me know what I owe you. Okay, Chaya, what were you saying?

Cashier: Have a nice day.

Customer: Bye, Chaya, talk to you later. Oh, were you talking to me again? Yes, sure, you too, thanks.

I can't become discouraged just because one person was multitasking and combining her shopping time with her social time. People are very busy. Although it was mortifying when I thought she was complimenting me; I can't believe I didn't see her headset. In fact, I was having a monologue, thinking we were communicating. I can certainly understand a busy person's need to have some social time. However, if she took a quick breath from her conversation long enough to notice and acknowledge my presence, it would certainly have been polite.

Maybe, this is part of what I'm supposed to learn in this field of work beyond trying to do mental math in a way that would make my fourth grade teacher beam with pride. And the good news is that there can be some real opportunities to help even in a job like this. And I'm sure that there will be many opportunities to help people in a variety of ways.

Here comes Libby. I have a lot of respect for her. Hello, Libby. Did you find everything okay?

Libby: Well, I'm a bit distracted and have a feeling that this may be one of those shopping trips where I bring home everything except what I came here to buy.

Cashier: That happens to all of us at times. Is there something specific that I can help you locate?

Libby: That's very nice of you. This work must be an adjustment for you. You seemed to have teacher written all over you.

Cashier: That's very kind of you to say. I'm experiencing some adjustment pains. I hope the distraction you mentioned is only about your involvement in many wonderful projects.

Libby: Actually, I feel bad because while I was speaking on my cell phone in your store, something I ordinarily don't do, I apparently offended a close friend in the process. Of course I apologized, yet here I was enjoying a special conversation with my sister and causing someone else discomfort unwittingly.

Cashier: Libby, it sounds like you usually take great pains to be respectful of people.

Libby: It's so interesting because I see this prevalent cell phone use as negative and impeding connections between people. Yet, when I received a special call, I picked it up enthusiastically and those sensitivities went out the window.

Cashier: It sounds like a human reaction when receiving a call from someone close to us. What's bothering you most about what happened?

Libby: I truly want to be a considerate person and I want people to think positively of me. And not only did I fail in this instance, I judged others who do the same thing as rude.

Cashier: I see. So it's far more than the cell phone, isn't it?

Libby: Yes, the cell phone just triggered this thought process.

Cashier: Libby, I can see this is really making you upset. You're clearly a person who strives to be one with her values. And, on the rare occasion that you err, it's really hard for you.

Libby: Exactly. I don't really give myself permission to make mistakes, especially not embarrassing ones in public.

Cashier: I hear you. I'm curious if these very high standards create hardships for you in other areas also?

Libby: Have you been watching through my window lately? There's so much tension from feeling that I'm walking on eggshells, always afraid I may crack one.

Cashier: That sounds so painful, like the smile on your face can be wiped away any time there's the slightest mistake.

Libby: Do you mean like with the cell phone? Well, you have to admit that was pretty terrible.

Cashier: Look, I can tell you that as a cashier, it's very unpleasant and often embarrassing when people continue with their conversations as if I don't exist. But a person who answers an occasional call, is she doing something terrible? The bigger question is, are we allowed to make mistakes, do our best to repair them, and move forward with a smile?

Libby: Are you suggesting I be a little more tolerant of myself?

Cashier: I couldn't have said it any better.

Libby: Well, you certainly gave me more than I what I shopped for. By the way, have you ever considered coaching?

19

PASSING THE BUCK

Basya Speaks:

'Twas the week before Pesach, and in the time-honored way of women worldwide during this season, I was sitting in my rocking chair, sipping coffee, and enjoying some leisure time. Ha! Just kidding. Burrowed inside my kitchen cabinets, the doorbell jarred me from my undignified position.

"Hi, Shiri, how are you?" I greeted the young woman at my door, anxious to be back in the kitchen.

"Baruch Hashem," she said quietly. "May I come in?"

Did I have a choice? Her eyes looked a bit misty, and I wondered what she needed. And with a sudden epiphany, I knew.

Shiri's husband had been unemployed for the last year, and she'd been flitting from job to job, desperately trying to support their family singlehandedly. And now with Yom Tov coming… My thoughts were traveling like a high-speed train racing down the tracks, and I knew what I had to do. Better to tell her right away so she knows to look elsewhere.

"We can't make Yom Tov," Shiri was saying, wiping her eyes. "I don't know what to do. And my landlord is threatening us with eviction."

That's really bad, I thought. I don't know anyone who's not having a houseful for Pesach who could just open their doors to a family of ten without blinking an eye.

"Can I get you a drink?" I offered, my eyes radiating sympathy.

"No. I can't drink, I can't eat. I need five hundred dollars by tomorrow," she pleaded. "Between that and my check, I should be able to handle this month's rent. Can you help me?"

"Shiri," I explained softly, "I'm in charge of *bikur cholim*. The funds I have can only be used for *bikur cholim* situations. I'm so sorry—"

"You don't understand," she interrupted. "I'm asking *you*. Personally. I'm desperate. Please, Basya."

Me? Us? The family that's always in the red? Is she joking? How I wish…

"Let me call my husband," I demurred, grabbing the phone and racing into a back room. I knew what he would say, but didn't know what else to do.

"We can give her twenty-five," my husband offered. "I wish we had more, but we just don't."

"I wish we could do more, Shiri," I explained, handing her the meager sum. "But I'm going to work on this. *B'ezras Hashem*, we'll get you the money."

I walked Shiri to the door, and the pain of her situation washed over me. Taking in her sagging shoulders and woebegone expression, I determined to raise the money. As soon as she left, I got on the phone. One of my first calls was to Raizy, in charge of the communal *tzedakah* fund. I poured the story into her listening ears.

"Basya," Raizy said, "Matnas Chinam has done all we can for Shiri's family at this point. We've given and given and simply don't have any more to pour into their family situation. I feel terrible, but there are other community needs as well."

My heart dropped into my stomach. Strike one. I leafed through our directory and began calling doctors' wives. Baruch Hashem, pledges began coming in.

"Who do I make the check out to?" they asked me. "We want it to be tax deductible."

"Oh, either to the Rabbi's discretionary fund or to Matnas Chinam would be fine," I answered quickly. Having used the Rabbi's fund in this way before, I figured either organization could then write a check from their account for Shiri's family, and everyone would be happy.

With Hashem's help, I collected not five but six hundred dollars in pledges — *mi k'Amcha Yisrael*! I felt accomplished and humbled at the same time; Hashem had placed this mitzvah in my hands, and He had enabled me to see it through to completion. Unfortunately, I didn't have all the money in hand by Shiri's deadline, and I nervously dialed her number.

"Don't worry," Shiri reassured me. "My son just paid our rent. With your help, I'll be able to pay the electric bill so they don't turn off our power. I can collect it after Shabbos."

I breathed a sigh of relief and resumed my preparations. Until the phone rang.

"Basya?"

"Oh, hi, Raizy."

"Did you tell the Kleinbergs to make out their check to Matnas Chinam, and then we would hand you a check for Shiri's family?"

"Yes," I answered.

"How could you do that?"

Huh?

"I told you we can't do any more for their family! How could you take that liberty without speaking to me? That is totally unacceptable."

"I — I'm sorry. I thought you couldn't help them directly from your fund. But I didn't know you would have a problem filtering the money if it came from outside sources. I've done that with the Rabbi's fund many times and never had an issue."

"Well, it's a big issue, and you've made it very sticky for me. I don't know what to do now."

"I'll just tell the Kleinmans to write their check to the Rabbi's fund. I'm sorry for the trouble."

Shaking, I hung up the phone and blinked back some tears. I felt somewhat dazed, unsure why I had just received that stinging slap. Here I had left my comfort zone to help a family of *ani'im* at an insanely busy time, and I get yelled at? By a *chesed* head, no less! How could she speak to me like that?

I took a few minutes to compose myself, and then I picked up the phone. I didn't want to bear a grudge, so I knew what I had to do.

"Raizy," I began, "I need to share something with you. All I did was try to help Shiri's family because they were desperate. I don't really understand why you got so upset. As I said, I've handled *tzedakah* money like that in the past and certainly meant no harm. I don't want to go into Yom Tov feeling hurt and angry, so I figured we could try to talk this through."

"I'm sorry," she conceded, although her tone didn't sound like it. "I didn't mean to hurt you. But I thought you understood that from our first conversation."

"If I understood," I countered, "then why would I have gone ahead and done this? After all these years, don't you know me a little better than that?"

"I'm sorry," she repeated, sounding more sincere this time.

"Okay," I sniffed. "I told a different *chesed* leader many years ago that if two *chesed* heads can't get along, we're in trouble." I waited to hear a chuckle, but there was silence. Oh, well. "Have a great Yom Tov."

"You, too," she said.

Hurt feelings continued to linger, and I struggled to find the message. I had tried so hard to help Shiri.

When Shiri came *motza'ei Shabbos*, she couldn't thank me enough. Her effusive appreciation soothed my wound.

"I'm so glad you came to me," I told her. "And I'm grateful I was able to help. *Berachah v'hatzlachah.*"

She gave me a warm hug and ran off with the envelope in hand.

Time has passed, and whenever I see Raizy, I smile warmly. But I can still taste the bitterness of that encounter…

Okay, Raizy, it's time to start with those affirmations the life coach recommended during your last session. Remember, the test of real learning is by application.

Being responsible for communal funds is a pressure, burden, and one of the most stressful jobs I have ever accepted.

Come on, Raizy, you can do better than that.

Okay, here goes take two: *Being responsible for communal funds is a privilege.*

Much better, now let's say it again as though you really mean it and feel it. Breathe in the privilege of helping others experiencing financial hardship. Exhale the toxicity of people whipping the messenger. Inhale the kindness and appreciation; exhale the anger at the irresponsible "do-gooders" who endanger our bookkeeping with their golden hearts and utter cluelessness at how the system needs to operate to remain viable. One final deep, cleansing breath, and stretch…

Oh, there's the phone. Calmness pervades every cell in my mind and body. "Why, hello Basya. How are you? It's lovely to hear from you during this pre-Pesach season. How can I help you?

"You would like to help Shiri? Basya, here's the problem. We only have a certain amount of resources, which need to be fairly allocated to each and every genuine need as determined by a board of rabbis who oversee our charity work. As much as Shiri's situation seems heart-wrenching, she's already received as much as we can justify giving her without taking away from other families that also deserve our help and also find themselves in exceedingly challenging situations.

"Thanks for your understanding, and I wish it could be different."

Why do I have this uncomfortable feeling that Basya, sensitive soul that she is, wasn't focused on the content of our conversation? It sounded like Shiri's plight really saddened her. She wouldn't take our procedures and change anything on her own, right? I don't need to worry, since I was very clear with her. Why do I feel that niggling feeling in my stomach?

There goes the phone again. It's our bookkeeper. I'm proud to say that all of our accounts are accurate and in keeping with the policies that our board of directors formulated. "Hello. Yes, this is Raizy. There's a problem with Shiri's account? I know for a fact that we didn't exceed the recommended amount for a family of her size with her financial constraints. Can you please show me the offensive paperwork, because something is wrong with this picture. We work so industriously to ensure that we have dotted every "i" and crossed every "t" to guarantee total transparency and follow-through with an organization of this nature.

"Someone sent a check with funds earmarked for Shiri? Why would anyone do that without consulting me?

It couldn't have been Basya, I think. *But I'll just call and check. I'm sure she wouldn't do that right after I explained the nature of our restrictions. Although, she was so caught up in Shiri's plight…there's only one way to find out.*

It was Basya! I'll work on forgiving her but I'll have to be firm and assertive this time because our organization can't afford to waste money on fines for breaking procedural policies. Even though she leads Bikur Cholim, she doesn't have any special privileges with these funds.

"Hello Basya, you didn't by any chance earmark funds for Shiri after we spoke, did you? You did?

"Basya, we're having major challenges with the bookkeeper now that you chose to follow your heart. I'm disturbed that you would choose to do this despite our earlier conversation. And without asking me first. I work very hard and even need special coaching so as not to send my blood pressure through the roof. I certainly don't like it when you take our carefully designed system and toss it in the garbage."

Later that evening Basya called again saying she was hurt? I'm scratching my head in utter befuddlement.

Affirmation time again. Go ahead, Raizy. *Being responsible for communal funds is a pressure, burden, and one of the most stressful jobs I have ever accepted…*

"PURR"FECTLY UNDERSTANDABLE

Hudis Speaks:

Atara comes over every Friday night unless she's out of town. An older single, with no one but a fluffy Persian cat for company, the allure of Shabbos and little bit of social interaction propel her through the hectic whirlwind of her workweek as a doctor. A lovely lady, brilliant, kind, warmhearted. But sometimes difficult. She likes to talk, to analyze, and doesn't like to be interrupted. However, we still have children home so interruptions are inevitable, and she scowls darkly whenever they happen.

One week Atara went out of town to visit some old friends

and asked us to feed Creampuff for a few days. We were happy to help.

On Sunday, my eight-year-old, Avi, was feeling somewhat down. He had found out about a birthday party he wasn't invited to, and his downturned lips and watery eyes said it all. I couldn't manage to boost his spirits, but then I had a brainstorm.

"Avi, Creampuff needs to be fed. Maybe you can even take him outside to play."

The sun rose in Avi's eyes, and suddenly he remembered that the world was a good place. Jumping up with newfound energy, he raced around the corner to Atara's house. *Pet therapy*, I mused, *it's like magic with the seniors in the assisted living home I work at, and it seemed to be spreading its light here, too.*

Avi stayed at Atara's for about an hour. At one point, he even brought Creampuff to my door; Creampuff looked content, dutifully wearing his collar and leash, and Avi was beaming and looking proud.

Later that day I sent Atara an email:

Hi, Atara,

I just want you to know how happy Avi was to take care of Creampuff today. He was feeling kind of low and really needed a boost, and pet therapy worked! They even went for a walk together! Hope you're enjoying your trip. We miss you.

Love,

Hudis

Atara's response wasn't long in coming:

Hudis,

Avi doesn't have permission to be in my house when I'm not home. In addition, Creampuff has a heart condition, and it's too hot for him to be taken outside. Avi needs to understand this.

Gulp. I must have read her note a dozen times. I sensed outrage that we had crossed a boundary and taken a liberty, and I was a bit nonplussed. How many years have we been friends? Who is the neighbor who keeps my key in case we get locked out? How many Shabbos meals have I served her? I thought our closeness transcended asking every little thing. If I had waited for an answer email as to whether or not Avi could go over, the time probably would have passed. And how should I have known she would object so strongly to Avi caring for the cat, especially when another child, in Avi's grade, often takes care of him?

I was angry and hurt, but decided to step back and examine my reaction. Who was right here? Well, granted, perhaps I should have asked before taking the liberty of sending Avi over. However, she could have used a much gentler tone, especially in light of the fact that we were doing her a favor by caring for her pet!

I decided to apologize for my part in the fiasco, assuring her that we would no longer allow Avi to care for Creampuff or to be in her house while she was away. But even as I typed the words, I felt wounded. What did she have against Avi, and why was it okay for the other little boy to do the same job?

I knew I should probably express my hurt feelings to Atara if I didn't want our friendship to suffer. But I was hesitant, not sure how she would take it, so I never said anything. Nor did I ever get over it.

Atara Speaks:

Work has been so pressured. Remind me, please, why I chose to be a doctor. What was I thinking? I have been looking forward to getting away and enjoying some vacation time with old friends, yet the only impediment is the anxiety of worrying about my cat's safety in my absence. Relaxing is only possible when I know he's safe with someone who understands him. It's hard to explain how an intelligent and accomplished doctor like myself carries such a deep attachment to this elderly, loyal cat, but it's something intangible that only an animal lover can comprehend. There is something very profound when he looks up at me with his soulful eyes that bespeak total devotion. Additionally, with my empty home, he is my daily companion — the giver and receiver of unconditional love.

This plan should be ironclad. My dear friend and neighbor, Hudis, can feed Creampuff daily and ensure that he doesn't escape. I can hire one of the neighborhood children who loves him to walk him daily. One cat lover recognizes another. The one potential pitfall in my plan is Avi, Hudis's eight-year-old son with big-time youngest-child syndrome, who thinks the world revolves around him and his whims. Why his behavior triggers me so strongly, I'll leave to the therapists, but if there's one person I absolutely don't trust around my cat, it's him. I'm wondering if there's a nice way to express this to Hudis, but I think I'll just have to trust her that she wouldn't leave Creampuff in her son's care even though she seems to give him everything else that he wants.

As much as I enjoy Hudis, and she so kindly opens her home, my loneliness sometimes screams out and I long for stimulating adult conversation. Every time the adult talk gets interesting and I'm reveling in the joy of being heard, their spoiled youngest child (who melts everyone's hearts but mine) steals the show, and I'm ready to pull out my hair. I know he's their youngest, but he's in third grade and should be capable of demonstrating some patience and respect at this point.

No matter what he does, it evokes a smile. A smile from his parents and siblings and a smile on my lips, yet a cringe on the inside.

Maybe on some level, I'm even jealous of that response.

When I talk and need listening, it appears that people's attention just drifts away, and I'm once again alone in the midst of people. This hurts more than being alone with my cat, when the expectations aren't there for reciprocal human interaction.

It's good to identify these feelings and go away with a clear head. Time to pack, Atara…

It's been a few days; time to check my e-mail. Oh, here's one from Hudis. Let's see what she has to say. I do miss that wonderful, kind lady.

What?! She let *him* walk my cat! Of all people! I thought I could trust her. The letdown hurts so much.

Hudis…

21

AND THE WINNER IS...

The Menaheles Speaks:

"Good morning, everyone, and welcome." I allowed my eyes to rove the room, taking a few moments to acknowledge everyone in attendance. "I'm excited to present a new idea for our students. We will be having a school-wide competition in basic Tanach knowledge. The students will have a month to prepare."

"A school-wide competition?" Mrs. Posen, a loyal and longtime teacher, interrupted, her tone sharp and cutting. "How can you do that? Do you realize what you'll do to their self-esteem? I thought our school prides itself on utilizing proper educational methods."

Her tirade continued, and it took all my strength to keep my face neutral and my lips clamped. How could she do this? Yell at the principal publicly, disagreeing so vehemently in front of rabbeim and *moros*?

Calling a fifteen-minute recess from our meeting, I stepped into my office to debrief. *What just happened?* I wondered, putting my head down on my desk as a sudden rush of fatigue overpowered me. Did Mrs. Posen really just explode like a volcano when I broached the idea of a school-wide competition? Is this cause for her termination?

My thoughts swirled in cyclonic upheaval, and I took a few deep breaths to stay my pounding heart. If she can lose control so quickly and easily, perhaps she can no longer be entrusted to nurture and mold the *neshamos* of our sweet, innocent third-graders. It is my job, first and foremost, to consider the educational needs of our children. Perhaps Mrs. Posen is ready for retirement and has lost what it takes to be in the classroom. In fact, maybe it's *bashert* that this first episode happened at a staff meeting and not in her classroom. This way we can handle it before any of our children are hurt. Not to mention the fact that she publicly berated me in front of the entire faculty. However, as a professional, I'd never allow personal feelings to get in the way of fulfilling my responsibilities. The real question is: Does Mrs. Posen serve as a role model and educator for our children and our staff? After this volatile outburst, I feared the answer might be no…

Come to think of it, I wondered what triggered her reaction. During the decade that Mrs. Posen had served as part of our faculty, she'd never conducted herself in the manner she displayed today. In fact, her students seem to genuinely like her, and their learning is on target with the curriculum. She encourages them when they're hesitant and praises their efforts. This was a strange deviation. Hmmm…could it be that she once had a terrible experience with a competition and that's why she feels so strongly? And even more, maybe she's trying to protect her students from suffering the pain that she experienced? That does put a different spin on things.

I'll have to explain to her the benefits of competition, and maybe she'll change her view, I thought. That is, if she's calm when we reconvene. I think I might take an Advil before going back. Okay, Menaheles, since practice makes perfect, imagine Mrs. Posen is right here in front of you. How would you endorse competition so she can see your point?

Mrs. Posen, thank you in advance for hearing me out. Competition can be a real learning experience for children, helping to prepare them for the real world. Isn't that the essence of chinuch? When they leave the safety of our daled amos, there will be college and careers around the bend. Their performances will be evaluated, and their levels of success may gain them status or financial remuneration. It isn't healthy to shield our children from what life will bring their way. We want them to have coping skills and be confident when confronted by life's challenges.

Yes, she'll surely see my point when I present it so logically. As far as her job, since this was a one-time aberration, I think I can overlook it this time, although I certainly hope she apologizes. But if it ever happens again…

Mrs. Posen Speaks:

Is it true that I, a veteran teacher, lost total control at the recent staff meeting? When the principal innocently brought up the words "school-wide competition," my blood began to boil and the words poured out almost involuntarily. It's a matter of principle, right? Doesn't everyone have areas about which they are very passionate, especially when it's a matter of potential harm to vulnerable children? The other staff members will need to think more carefully before nodding in acquiescence at every new project that may bring PR to the school without a careful evaluation of the consequences. So we may have state winners and get extra funding, but at what cost?

I took a deep breath and tried to calm myself. *Look in the mirror, dear teacher. Passion about ideas doesn't usually yield emotional explosions and a total resistance to hearing any dissenting opinions. What happened to listening to other ideas and considering their merits? Flexibility? Negotiation? Win-win solutions? Modeling the behavior we want to teach? Out of the window in your fit of rage...*

This wasn't a normal response from me. *What's really going on?* I decided to open the window within and take a deep breath.

I could picture the day in my mind, even though getting the salutatorian award instead of being the valedictorian happened over thirty years ago. That wound can't still be festering — or can it? And then when my kids were young, it hurt when I wasn't invited to the honor-roll breakfasts. My children weren't wired to be angelic students. Yet somehow I internalized this as my parental failure. Furthermore, how many graduations did I attend when most of the parents and students cringed as just a select few, as determined by the staff, merited public acknowledgement? Oh, there's so much personal pain here. I have to acknowledge it honestly. Only then can I deal with it rather than suppress it and pretend it will go away. I wonder how much experience shapes my opinions as opposed to just intellectual research.

Research can generally go both ways. I'm unapologetic for my stance, yet filled with remorse for my outburst. I need to return to the staffroom for a real conversation where we can explore the benefits and the risks to competition in school, emotions aside.

22

A TELLING MOMENT

Kayla Speaks:

Busy having a blast in high school, I had important things on my agenda, like reveling in my large part in our upcoming play, maintaining my A average, and keeping up with my friends — which was a job in itself. Endowed with a naturally outgoing, extroverted personality, I thrived on social interaction — lots of it. It nourished my soul much like my three meals a day sustained my body. Yet over the past few months, I had been feeling distinctly unwell. Slightly nauseous with some recurrent abdominal pain, I kept putting it on the back burner; who had time to be sick? And why worry my mother when it was probably just a call for extra rest and less stress? But when my symptoms began to get worse and I could no longer hide the way I was feeling, my mother's antennae began twitching, and off we went to our family practitioner. Dr. R. took copious notes, examined me, and when the results of the blood work came in a few days later, so did his unwelcome call.

"Take her to the hospital," he told my mother. "Immediately."

When my mother picked me up early from school and delivered her bombshell, my world imploded.

"Now?" I squeaked. "But I have play practice today!"

"Kayla, I'm so sorry," she said, squeezing my hand reassuringly. "I know how hard this is. But we may be dealing with something that needs medical attention, and if we don't get it under control, it can get worse, quickly. We have no choice."

I glanced at my mother, whose face looked white, and my heart dropped. *The hospital? Me? Was I dreaming? And what exactly were they afraid I had?* Terrified, I didn't ask. *Maybe if I didn't ask, it wouldn't become reality…*

Several days later we had our diagnosis: Crohn's disease.

"Hopefully the medication will manage it, and you can continue with your regular lifestyle and activities," the nurse assured me as she signed my discharge papers.

Hopefully? The dubious word dangled tenuously in my mind as I made a sudden dash for the bathroom. My mother's anxiety was thick and tangible, and I could feel her eyes boring into my back before I slammed the door.

■ ■ ■

WITH HASHEM'S HELP, YEARS HAVE passed since my initial diagnosis, and my Crohn's has been eminently manageable. That memorable hospitalization was my only one. Sure, I had the occasional flare-up that required some consultation and medical intervention. Switching medications or a new dose consistently remedied the problem, and no one was able to look at me and see a girl with a serious condition. I kept up with the best of 'em. I attended a prestigious Israeli seminary and returned all fired up, ready to embark on the next new and exciting stage of my life: *shidduchim*.

My mother got on the phone and dutifully sent off my résumé to several *shadchanim*. On paper I was a top girl — an excellent student, sterling *middos*, sociable, and wanting a serious *ben Torah* with whom I could share my life. However, a large question danced in front of our eyes, demanding an answer, a question too large for us to take on our shoulders. Seeking clear guidance, we consulted a *posek*.

"As long as her Crohn's is under control," we were told unequivocally, "especially since it's been several years since her initial flare-up, it may be kept under wraps until the third date."

"But isn't that deceitful?" I asked my parents, struggling with the idea.

"We have a *psak*," my parents assured me, "so we know we're walking the straight path."

Shalom and I went out, and our first two dates felt like a dream. *But how would he react to my news*, I worried, carefully applying my makeup before date number three. Would he feel deceived? Maybe he would have refused to go out with me had he known about my situation. After all, on paper, my résumé was top-notch. But in reality, there was an insidious illness lurking within my body that could potentially flare up at any time and cause untold complications… *Hashem, if Shalom is the right boy for me, please make sure he's okay with this.*

Straightening my skirt, I peered into the mirror once more as the doorbell rang. I couldn't help but wonder how I'd feel if someone had concealed such vital information from me. Honest self-reflection told me I'd be furious, feeling deceived and betrayed. *Will he drop me? Will anyone want me? Don't cry,* I ordered myself as I slowly descended the stairs. *It will ruin your makeup!*

Shalom Speaks:

Yes, Rebbi, I really like Kayla. I felt comfortable with her from the very first date, and we seem to have common interests and goals. In the past, the pressure to make conversation and to review the list of topics before each date consumed my attention. With Kayla, our conversations flow so naturally, and I enjoy listening to her comments and questions. At the end of both dates, I left feeling that we haven't run short of topics to discuss."

"It sounds like you didn't come with any question, Shalom. Continue with this *shidduch* and *hatzlachah* in achieving clarity as you proceed."

Just like the past two dates, the third was enjoyable, and I could only see wonderful traits in Kayla.

"Thank you, Kayla, for a very nice evening."

"Before we call it a night, I have something I need to tell you." She looked nervous.

"Sure, what's on your mind?"

"This isn't easy for me to say. When I was in high school, I was diagnosed with Crohn's disease. It was a shock to all of us, but baruch Hashem has been well under control since I learned how to manage it. I eat very nutritiously and prioritize regular exercise. Please understand that it wasn't our intention to deceive you by waiting until now to inform you. Our *rav* told us this is the correct procedure. You'll probably need time to think."

"Um, Kayla, will you excuse me for a few moments, please?"

Bolting from the table, I made a beeline for the restroom, my insides heaving. *How could they do this to me?!* Everything was going so smoothly, a mazal tov seemed possible, and now...

I felt terribly disturbed and deceived. It's very nice to quote *daas Torah*, but they're dealing with feelings here! Who knows if I would have agreed to go out with her had I known this information from the get-go? There were plenty of other résumés waiting...

I don't want to be a nurse to my wife! What if she gets sick?

Come now, Shalom, does anyone ever know what they're signing up for?

Hmm, good point.

Kayla's waiting. What will you tell her? Are you ready to call it quits?

I don't know. I'm angry and hurting right now.

I understand. But try to think of it from her point of view.

Well, okay...

I took a few deep breaths, tried to deescalate my blood pressure, and made a decision. If Kayla were my sister, I would have totally understood the route she and her family took. And therefore, I think I'm willing to continue with this *shidduch*. There's too much potential to simply toss away the opportunity.

I walked back to where Kayla was waiting; she was surely expecting the worst. My heart melted, and I davened for the right words.

"This discovery must have really shaken you up and been a very difficult challenge."

Tears filled her eyes, and spilled onto her cheeks. "I'm sorry. I didn't mean to start crying." She quickly brushed away the tears.

"Did I say something wrong? I'm sorry if I upset you."

"No, you responded so empathetically. I'm just relieved."

If she only knew...

"You thought I might get angry and walk away in a cloud of thunder. I haven't done that since I was nine. At that age, my tantrums could be heard from across the street. Remind me later to tell you that story."

We talked a bit more about her condition and how it affected her, how she felt when she found out. I decided I needed to call my Rebbi again. He always puts things into perspective.

"Look, this is a big decision," I told her, "which I'll need to discuss with my parents and my Rebbi. But, honestly, I was afraid there was something worse. If Hashem thinks we're suited for one another, which I hope is the case, something tells me we'll figure this out together."

Kayla provided her doctor's number. My parents will undoubtedly want more information about Crohn's to gain a better understanding of this condition. I admire the way she accepted a challenge and didn't let it interfere with her goals. She adopted a very healthy lifestyle and in some ways may be even healthier than most due to this.

I gave her a call later that night.

"Kayla, would you like to hear my tantrum story? At nine years old, some boys in my class enjoyed making fun of me. They called me names and ran away, observing my volcanic eruption from a corner. It took a long time and the help of a wonderful school counselor to teach me that my angry reactions were encouraging the very behavior that upset me so much.

"As a sensitive child, it was hard to realize that I was merely a puppet in their hands and would explode or cry at their whim. When I learned tools that empowered me to choose how to respond to provocation, interestingly enough, the bullying stopped. I promised myself that one day I'd help children struggling with similar issues.

"I chose a yeshivah that really stresses interpersonal relationships and emphasizes *mussar*, and it's gratifying to know that my friends consider me easygoing.

"So, Kayla, when you looked at me so nervously tonight, I remembered these lessons from childhood. My goal is to be the kind of guy who makes people feel safe as they communicate what's on their mind, even if it might be a loaded topic. And, this may be premature to say, but I'm very interested in hearing your thoughts and feelings.

"Is there any part of me that wished I knew this from the beginning? Yes.

"Do I understand that you were following a halachic ruling and respect that?" I paused for a moment, took a deep breath, and continued. "Yes again."

"Do I appreciate the courage that it took for you to tell me directly and not through a middle person? Very much.

"Am I angry with you or at your parents? Not at all. (Well… let's just say I'm working on it. But it's okay to change the truth for *darchei shalom*, isn't it?) As a matter of fact, I respect you and value the fact that you trusted me to share something private.

"Well, Kayla, your parents are probably pacing, wondering how this conversation is proceeding. I'll let you go and we'll be in touch in a few days."

23

PURIM DELIGHTS

Rena Speaks:

It's that time of year again — time to start thinking about *mishloach manos*. With two children in Israel, including one married couple with a baby and one daughter in seminary, I'd love to spice up their Purim by ordering them something nice to show them how much we miss them and think about them. But I also don't want to spend too much. Hmm…money always seems to be at the root of my dilemmas.

Oh, look at that! A company called Purim Delights just emailed me, wondering if I need their services this year. I think I used them once before a few years ago when a different daughter was in seminary. I'll just shoot off a quick response and see if they can do something for both kids that can work within my budget.

Meanwhile, the pace of life is picking up, and I'm feeling pressured by jobs coming at me from all sides. One child's camp application is due, and they want the health form included or they won't look at her application, which means I have to run the form to the doctor and wait for it to be returned before I can send it out. The day school said registration must be completed *now*, and in the meantime, our small Purim *seudah* is growing by the day. We started off as eight people, and we've increased to fifteen. And I need to start baking for *mishloach manos*. Okay, Rena, calm down. You're one person and you can only do one job at a time. You'll get it all done. Deep breath, write a list, and tackle each job. Oh my, the deadline for my Purim story is three days from now? HELP!

■ ■ ■

PHEW! I GOT THE STORY out, and the health form has been delivered to our pediatrician. So we're making some progress, baruch Hashem. Now why hasn't Purim Delights responded? It's been a few days already. I guess they can't work within my budget. Okay, I'll try a different company. I really need to get this settled; there's so much to do and so little time to get everything done. There, Marvelous Munchies said they can definitely send packages to both my girls, and they can do it for the price I requested. Baruch Hashem, the order is taken care of, and that's one more thing I can cross off of my list.

Uh-oh. Purim Delights just emailed me. They are happy to send both packages, and can do it for the price I requested. I feel bad, but I have to tell them I took my business elsewhere because

I didn't hear from them soon enough. I wish I could order from them, too, but that would really defeat my purpose of trying to keep the cost down. Maybe I should have emailed them first and told them that I needed this taken care of within a certain time frame? I hope they won't be too upset.

Upset wasn't the word. Mrs. Purim Delights told me she was surprised that I didn't wait for her reply. Don't I remember, she asked, when she went out of her way a few years ago to keep the price within my budget when I made an order for my daughter in seminary? Gulp. I hate conflict. I certainly wasn't trying to upset her, take business away from someone who was counting on it, nor did I want to show a lack of *hakaras hatov* for a previous favor. I just needed to get the job done, and I hadn't heard back from her. Turns out she just made a wedding and fell a little behind in her emails. So did I make a mistake? I certainly upset another person, so right or not, I'll apologize. Perhaps I'll be clearer in my communication the next time so that such a scenario won't happen again. And perhaps, dear Self, patience is a virtue. On the other hand, this is business, and aren't I entitled to a clear response in an efficient manner so that I can make my order? Ah, who knows? (Hashem, did I goof or not?) Hopefully next time will be better.

What a beautiful *simchah*! It's hard to believe that our oldest daughter is married. When people told me that the years would fly, I remember smiling politely and wondering if they understood that every sleepless night felt like an eternity. Somehow they were wiser than I recognized. Sometimes I wonder why Hashem didn't pair the energy and exuberance of youth with the wisdom of age and experience. It's almost as if we need to enter a new stage as a wide-eyed beginner. Just like with the wedding preparations, I had no idea how all-encompassing it would be. Somehow, I naively believed that I could keep on top of my workload and make a *simchah* simultaneously. I failed to consider the emotional exhaustion, the placement for over forty out-of-town guests, the week of *sheva berachos*, and the seemingly endless errands attending to every detail. And of course, trying to keep the *kallah* calm while my own tension was sky-high. Anyway, there will be time for musing later. Now it's the busiest time of year for beautiful Purim creations, and every sale will assist us in paying off the debts from this wedding.

I feel fortunate to have work that expresses my creativity and helps people fulfill a mitzvah. Purim is such a joyful time, enabling us to give that extra thought about the people we're so grateful to have in our lives and rise above some of the petty disagreements that inevitably arise. Okay, now to check the e-mails and orders and get to work. Amazing! Look how many e-mails with orders accumulated just over this week. I guess the stage of sleepless nights may be recurring. Thank you, Hashem, for sending me customers who can value my talent. Every person needs to be appreciated for her special gifts.

One sizzling coffee, one telephone, and one computer ready to take the orders. And one enthusiastic woman ready to give individualized attention and style to each customer. That is my vision and my mission. No two relationships are the same. Therefore, customizing every *mishloach manos* to capture a unique flavor of the connection adds that intangible touch that strengthens the warm feelings between people. What a privilege to do this work, but here I go musing again. It's not like me to become so emotional over my everyday tasks. It must be the aftermath of the wedding. My mascara runneth over. Oh well, I guess masks are popular in this season!

I opened an e-mail from a returning client and responded in the affirmative; we would be able to meet her needs. Within seconds, however, my inbox pinged — apparently I was too late in responding; she had taken her business elsewhere. I responded by explaining the situation, the wedding, being busy… I mean, she couldn't wait three days? She didn't seem to remember the strings I pulled for her the last time she asked. Is there no loyalty anymore?

Well, it appears that even customers I gave special discounts to in the past became impatient when I didn't respond within a few days of their query. Although I can own my mistakes and strive for better service in the future, I still feel pained. Where is their loyalty to the service and quality I provide? It hurts deeply, emotionally as well as financially. My husband and I were counting on these funds for wedding expenses. Well, there are still some customers on the list. After hearing ten people echo the same sentiments about regretfully taking their business elsewhere, I'm ready for a positive infusion. This next lady on the list surely waited for me. She sounded so kind and considerate. She wouldn't be so quick to go elsewhere after all the extra effort I put into serving her the last time.

Hello, long time, no speak. How are you and your family? I'm pleased to inform you that I can provide for you in the price range you are seeking and quality won't be compromised.

You went elsewhere… I know I sound upset. I am. It's difficult for me to understand that just because we were zocheh to marry off a child and I got a bit behind in my e-mails, my customers moved on. I thought there was much more of a relationship. And I thought that in our circles, people understand all the different responsibilities we juggle.

Yes, it's true that everyone is busy. I'm sorry for losing it with you.

It's just an accumulation of frustration, maybe predominantly with myself. Okay, no hard feelings and have a nice Purim.

Well, at least I have ten orders, and more may come from some last-minute planners.

This isn't the mental state I wanted to have right before the Purim season. All of this anger and resentment will just poison my heart. Can it be that there is more validity to the other side than I realized?

As a business owner, should I have hired a girl to supervise the e-mails and respond so that customers felt reassured their orders were being processed? Perhaps I'm being unrealistic. Many businesses that are open one year close the next year — and then these customers would be in a difficult spot, with insufficient time to get in their Purim orders. No one wants to send *mishloach manos* after the fact. Clearly there are many people who appreciate my work. That is a huge blessing. Yes, it would have been nice to have everyone standing in line waiting for me. But am I being just a tad unrealistic in today's frantically paced society and at the busiest time of the year? The last woman in particular seems like she never wanted to hurt anyone and was almost surprised to hear from me. It appears she inferred that I couldn't accommodate her this year.

Yes, Purim is a time to strengthen relationships. I can only change myself and I need to work on being more attuned to my customers' feelings of urgency. Maybe with the extra time that I now have, I can send each of my customers a special creation just to show there are no hard feelings and that it would be a privilege to serve them in the future.

What a powerful Purim lesson I learned this year. Providing this valuable service for my customers is a serious commitment, one they need to be able to trust. Okay, a fresh cup of coffee, a new coat of mascara, and a positive mindset. Purim, here we come!

24

TRIANGULAR TRAUMA

Leah Speaks:

So every time I see a policeman, I freeze, and those traumatic memories get dredged up in my mind. I was arrested, torn from my family, and thrown behind bars for a full thirty hours, and I hadn't done anything wrong! The whole thing was such an insidious mess. But I've been permanently traumatized, and I shake every time I see a police car, not to mention an officer in the flesh. I'm so tired of reliving the situation on such a regular basis. It's over, so why I can't I just move past it? Can you help me?"

My client looked at me pleadingly, and my heart melted for her pain. Hmmm…I tapped my fingers on my desk, deep in thought. She had already come to my office several times, and we had made real headway with her situation, however, she was still highly distressed. Perhaps suggesting an adjunct tool could help enhance the pace of her progress and sense of healing. "You know," I told her thoughtfully, "I have a friend who specializes in hypnosis. Does that sound like something you'd be willing to try?"

"I'll do anything," Lisa assured me, and I saw the pain flicker in her eyes.

"Let me call her now and see if she can fit you into her schedule."

Lisa waited patiently while I contacted Elisheva. "No problem," Elisheva assured me. "Ask her if tomorrow at eleven will work for her?"

"So you're all set," I told Lisa, smiling as I walked her to the door. "Let me know how it works for you, and I'll see you next week."

Admittedly, I harbored a secret fear that I tried to squelch. What if Lisa likes Elisheva better than me? What if they connect on a deeper level and I become obsolete as Lisa's therapist? And it will be all my doing! Imagine the owner of Kroger directing a customer to Publix for a better shopping experience! The proprietor of Ladies' Workout Express sending a potential client to L.A. Fitness because they have more up-to-date equipment…Why, surely they would have to be seized by temporary insanity to jeopardize their own business! So why did I just send Lisa to another practitioner, pray tell?

The answer is resoundingly clear, and I recognize its clarion call of truth. Ultimately, I have my patients' best interests in mind, and I want to help this particular woman conquer her fear and put it behind her. As of yet, she requires more healing. Hypnosis may be the tool that helps her internalize messages of safety and well-being on a very deep level beyond what we touch with conventional talk therapy. A wave of calm washed over me as I reassured myself that I had acted properly, truly *l'Sheim Shamayim*.

"Oh, hi, Lisa, how did it go? Are you calling to schedule our next session? Let me look at my calendar, pl—, what did you say? We won't be continuing anymore? Why, has something happened? Oh, you really connected to Dr. Elisheva and feel it would be more beneficial for you to continue your sessions with her? I understand, of course. The main thing is that you've found the proper conduit to help you achieve your goal. I'm very happy for you, Lisa. Yes, I wish you the very best."

I hung up the phone and stared sightlessly ahead. I know I did the right thing, but somehow that knowledge was providing scant comfort to the wound in my soul. Isn't Elisheva supposed to be my friend? Why didn't she redirect Lisa back to my office? Doesn't she care about me? I'd never take away her clients… Oh, come on, Leah. *Parnassah* is *min haShamayim*. You know that. This isn't Elisheva's fault; it's simply the Master Conductor's plan. Sigh. Nope, not there yet. Maybe I'll call Elisheva and see if she can squeeze me in for some hypnosis…

Elisheva Speaks:

"Sure Leah, thanks for thinking of me. It would be a pleasure to team up and work together to help a client." I decided to research trauma and locate some really effective scripts to help create inner peace and relaxation. It's exciting to share a client with my special friend.

Within just a few sessions Lisa had major breakthroughs.

"Lisa, I'm amazed by your progress. It appears you're no longer haunted by your fear of police. It's been a delight working with you and I wish you continued success. Would you be comfortable sharing what you found most helpful?"

She looked at me. "Well, so many aspects contributed to the picture, let me gather my thoughts. Firstly, I felt comfortable with you immediately as well as a sense of confidence that you would be able to help me. Secondly, the deep breathing and ability to relax is something so new for me. I seem to be a perpetual engine rarely pausing and allowing myself the chance to pause, reflect, and relax in the moment. In that place of the present moment, breathing in your suggestions of safety and security, I was able to let go of my fear. How can I thank you?"

"You just did! I'm so gratified that you responded so well to the hypnosis. Please send Leah my warmest regards when you see her the next time."

"Actually, I'm planning to call Leah. She's a lovely person and I definitely gained from my work with her. But finding the right therapist is like a *shidduch*. And, I'll be forever grateful to her for leading me to you. As I can't afford to see two therapists, I'd like to continue working on issues relating to personal growth with you."

"I'm honored by your willingness to trust me and work with me," I said, "but please understand that Leah and I are friends with tremendous regard for one another on a professional level as well. There is an understood protocol that we don't take each other's clients."

"I understand Leah is a very spiritual person," Lisa said. "I'm convinced she'll be happy if I can get more help from you. In fact, I'll call her today and let her know of my decision. Even if you refuse to see me, I won't be returning to see Leah. Now that I've experienced a method that offers such quick results and helped me so deeply, I can't return to the other methods with the same motivation. It wouldn't be fair to Leah or me."

I felt uncomfortable with how the conversation was progressing. "Let's speak tomorrow, to give me some time to process your sentiments. Again, congratulations on your hard work. Ultimately, the therapist is only a facilitator. It was your willingness that affected your healing of the trauma. Be well and all the best."

This was an unexpected development. I gave Lisa the benefit of every tool in my arsenal out of love for my friend and colleague — and I'd caused Leah to lose a client. Leah will feel hurt and betrayed even if I don't continue seeing Lisa. There must be a lesson somewhere. It's so hard to know what the right step is to take. I need to reach out to Leah and reassure her that this was never my intention. She is such a true friend. I truly hope our friendship can withstand this challenge. I wonder if our roles were reversed, would I find it in my heart to give her my blessings. Would I be able to trust her again?

This is truly agonizing. One part of my heart is filled with joy that I helped a client heal from a trauma that has been destroying her peace of mind. The other part is aching for the pain that I unwittingly caused to my friend. Maybe, I'll call Leah for some of her emotionally focused interventions.

25

THOSE ARE THE BRAKES

Meir Speaks:

It was right before *bein hazemanim* when Yitzy Sugarman asked me the favor. He's been my best friend since the third grade. His family wanted to go on a Chol HaMoed outing, but didn't have much money to play with. So Yitzy had an idea.

"Meir, you know my father's been out of work for a long time, right?"

"Right."

"So I was wondering, you're going back home anyway. And my family was talking about going to Silver Lake Trail, but renting bikes is kind of pricey. So I thought, well, maybe I could borrow your bike until you get back."

"Sure," I agreed, "I'm going home anyway. No problem. Enjoy."

I hope he's careful with it. But how could I say no? I've asked him to lend me so many things, and he always says yes…

The Sugarmans were thrilled; all the kids had been able to borrow bikes. Yitzy couldn't thank me enough. But when I came back and got on my bike, something was wrong. The brakes weren't working well, and a strange noise sounded each time I tried to pick up speed.

"Did anything happen while you had the bike?" I asked Yitzy.

"No, it rode fine," Yitzy assured me. "Thanks for letting me use it. There was a funny kind of noise when I rode really fast, but other than that, it was perfect."

Why in the world, I wondered, *did you keep riding if you heard a strange noise? You should have called me or gotten it checked out. No wonder it's broken!*

Somewhat disconcerted, I took it to the bike shop. I had been generous and tried to do a mitzvah, but it backfired.

"Three hundred dollars," the repairman said, "and we'll have it just like new. But next time," he warned, wagging his finger, "if you hear something unusual, bring it in right away. It's possible that we could have simply tightened the brakes instead of having to replace them."

Gee, thanks. I called Yitzy and told him what happened.

"I'm so sorry," Yitzy said. But he didn't offer compensation.

What good does sorry do if you're not going to help pay for damage that you caused?

I didn't know what to do. I did know that I was absolutely furious. He ruined my bike! But he can't afford the repair. After all, Rabbi Sugarman lost his job a year ago. Who says I can afford the repair? I don't have three hundred dollars just lying around. Plus, I shouldn't have to pay for this! My bike isn't a luxury for me; I go everywhere on it. Thoroughly confused, I finally decided to ask my *rosh yeshivah* for advice. Why Yitzi didn't feel the need to ask *daas Torah* was beyond me.

The *rosh yeshivah*'s words were priceless.

"*Mitzad hadin*, you're right. Yitzy was negligent and owes you the money to cover the repair. However, I want you to tell them that I said they're *patur*."

Reaching into the drawer of his large, mahogany desk, the *rosh yeshivah* pulled out an envelope. With a flourish, he handed me three hundred dollars.

"I have a special fund for these types of situations," he confided. "Please keep this between us." Putting a finger on his lips, he gave me a conspiratorial wink.

I have even more respect for the *rosh yeshivah* now; what a tzaddik! But that Yitzy... I'm still annoyed by his lack of owning up. From what the bike repairman said, he should have realized something was wrong before it got so bad. So am I still best friends with him? I don't know, I'll have to think about it. I need a best friend I can trust.

"Ma, can't we do anything exciting on Chol Hamoed? You should hear what the guys do and it becomes the talk of the yeshivah for days. Real exciting stuff. I'm tired of being told there's no money for any fun in this family." I let out a sigh hoping that my complaining would pay off, but I knew perfectly well that trips weren't a priority right now.

"Yitzy, I know this situation is tough on you and everyone in the family. Believe me, Tatty and I would love to give our children everything that is good for them. Actually, we did plan an outing this Chol HaMoed that you'll love. There's a beautiful new bike trail, and we thought we could all go riding together and then have a picnic."

"I do enjoy biking, Mom, but you're forgetting something. All of us have outgrown our bikes by miles."

"I thought you could each borrow for one day. Chances are the other families won't be using them at the same time. You guys are very responsible and will take good care of them. Isn't your friend Meir going away for Yom Tov? You've loaned him our stuff more times than I can count. I'm sure he'd be happy to return the favor."

I perked up right away. Meir would definitely lend me his bike, and he has always been such a great friend. "Okay, Mom, that does sound like a nice plan, and Mom, sorry for complaining. I know you do your best for us. Just sometimes, it's tough being the only one of the guys feeling left out of what sounds like a really good time."

"I hear you, Yitzy, and accept your apology. You can feel proud of how maturely you have been handling this challenge in general, and hopefully our situation will improve, with Hashem's help."

"Mom, I'm going to head over to Meir's right now to check out this bike idea."

I ran there as quickly as I could, and as I had suspected, he was more than happy to help.

"Yitzy, I'd be happy to loan you my new 12-speed bike. If there is any guy who's trustworthy, it's you. I can't even count the amount of times you loaned me your stuff and bailed me out when I didn't have what I needed. Enjoy the bike, courtesy of Uncle Stan. It was thanks to his big check that I got that bike. And have a great Yom Tov. The bike is in great shape, enjoy it."

"Thanks, Meir. It's awesome."

I didn't know if I'd ever admit this to the *chevrah*, but bike riding was great. I loved racing down the paths and feeling so free. The truth was that I wasn't really wild over roller coasters, but I didn't say it publicly. What kind of wimp got a queasy stomach on a roller coaster or worse, dared to be scared?

What was that noise coming from the bike? That didn't sound normal. Meir always told me I worry too much. Didn't he just say it was in great shape? It was probably nothing. It sure didn't sound like nothing, though.

I wondered if I should mention this noise to Tatty. If I did, he'd feel a need to pay for repairs and it would be my fault. I knew the financial struggle we were having. If I didn't mention it and pretended it was a normal noise, wasn't I cheating my best friend? Why was everything in life so complicated?

It's possible that Meir didn't realize that something wasn't working properly before he loaned it to me. Who said it was my fault? I sure didn't mistreat it. Maybe Meir, scatterbrain that he is, wouldn't even notice it till the next time he needed a tune-up, and then it wouldn't cost any extra money. I thought, *Yitzy, my boy, you got a winner*. Bottom line is, as much as I prided myself for being a *mentsch*, I must not burden my parents any more. They were suffering enough. I remembered Mommy's face when I exploded a few days ago. Every time I closed my eyes, I saw her pain.

This time, as much as I wanted to be a good friend, I was choosing to be a good son.

What noise from the bike? This bike is a beauty, in great working order, just like Meir said. He certainly is the expert of his own bike. "Come on, guys, race you to the field where we can have a great game of baseball."

After Yom Tov I got the call that I had been dreading.

"Oh, hi, Meir. Did I notice anything funny when I rode your bike? Three hundred dollars? Oh, wow! Thanks so much for lending it to me though. It was amazing."

I started worrying, my thoughts going in circles. *I probably have a shailah on my hands. But what if the Rav says I have to pay? We don't have the money! Meir has two working parents; they can probably afford it. I'm sure Hashem wouldn't want me to stress my parents out by telling them we owe three hundred dollars. No, it's definitely better to keep quiet and put this whole thing behind us. I just hope it wasn't my fault…*

26

THE EXTRA MILE

Yocheved Speaks:

Shevi and I had been friends forever. We walked each other through minor and major tribulations of raising our families, always there for each other. But during the last few years, our relationship became more one-sided. After years of roller-coaster riding in a tumultuous marriage, Shevi and Mordechai finally divorced. Shevi needed a lot of support to get through that trying time, especially when Mordechai remarried shortly after the *get* was finalized.

Time passed, and Shevi moved on, literally and figuratively.

Packing up her house of almost twenty years, she decided to move to Passaic and create a new life for herself. With Hashem's help, her new *bashert* awaited her there, and several months after her move, she called me with a jubilant mazal tov.

"It would mean the world to me if you came to my wedding," she told me. How could I not go? I'm not a big traveler and flights are expensive, but what don't you do for a lifetime friend?

Two weeks before the wedding, I left her a message that I had a ticket.

"I can't wait to see you!" she texted me.

A text? Can't she even pick up the phone and tell me that I made her day?

Assuming she would arrange for my transportation to and from the airport as we out-of-towners regularly do for our guests when making a *simchah*, I waited to hear who would be picking me up. When no message was forthcoming, I finally called her.

"Shevi, do you have someone who can get me from the airport?" I asked.

"I really don't know anyone I can ask," she replied, casually shrugging off the responsibility.

My temper started to flare, and I struggled to keep my voice neutral. Why couldn't she ask her *chasan* if he knew anyone? Or at least offer to handle the expense if I had to get a taxi? After all, she was marrying someone who had a lucrative job.

"Shevi, I can't really afford to pay a taxi on top of my airline ticket," I pressed. "So I'm not sure what to do now."

Finally, she got the hint and arranged for a car service to pick me up, splitting the cost with me. I felt she should have covered the whole tab, but I let it go and thanked her graciously.

The wedding was poignant and beautiful, and I was so glad that I was able to be there with her. Watching her summon the strength to leave her tattered past behind and step into a hopeful future, I could only wipe my streaming eyes and daven as I gazed at her standing beside her new husband under a simple *chuppah*.

The next day, the same car service spirited me back to the airport, and in short order I found myself back home and thankfully reimmersed in my routine. Every so often I'd think about Shevi and wonder how she was managing, but we didn't talk much over the next few months. Assuming she was busy building her new home, I didn't take it too personally when my calls weren't returned. And then the call came.

"Yocheved, I'm coming in for Robin's wedding," Shevi informed me.

Robin was a mutual friend of ours, and we were both thrilled that she had finally met her *bashert* after a long, painful search.

"Great!" I said, excited that we'd have a chance to reconnect.

"I was wondering," she continued, "do you think you could give Betzalel and me a ride back to the airport on Sunday?"

Now, now, Yocheved, simmer down. You know nekamah is a no-no. Simply because she had to be practically coerced to help you with your airport transportation when you were coming in for her simchah isn't an excuse to say no to her request. You know that, right?

"Let me check my schedule and get back to you," I told her, needing some time to formulate my response.

Since I didn't want *nekamah* to be on my list of *aveiros*, although I admit I was somewhat tempted, I knew I'd say yes. However, since my children were off on Sunday, I didn't want to take them in the middle of the day and disrupt our whole schedule.

"I can take you earlier than you need to go," I offered, "but I have to be home by 1:30."

Shevi hemmed, double-checking that I couldn't take them any later, and wound up getting another friend to give them a ride so they wouldn't have to hang out for hours at the airport. I breathed a sigh of relief, feeling I had done my part yet maintained a healthy boundary.

I imagined what I'd say to her if I had the courage. *Shevi, I'll always love you and wish only good things for you. But once upon a time we were there for each other. And I miss that.*

Shevi Speaks:

Who would have believed, after all the turmoil, that I'd get another chance at happiness with such a wonderful guy? I must share this news with Yocheved. She really stood by my side through each and every excruciating part of my journey.

Amazing! It sounds like Yocheved will come to the wedding. I'm so totally overwhelmed making a wedding in a new city. It is so different this time around, when I'm not just the prop and parents deal with all the technical details. Now, I'm the bride and the wedding planner. I wish I had a friend like Yocheved locally who could hold my hand through all the details and squeeze when needed.

Emotionally, everything is also so different this time around. The first time, I entered naively with the assumption that people who get married stay married and live happily ever after. Now, after having gone through turbulence, I feel scared. I'm also worried about the children. Will this new marriage affect them negatively? I always want them to feel welcome in my home. Some children feel they have no home when their parents remarry and wonder about where they fit into the equation. Isn't it amazing that more homes can mean less sometimes?

How can I cope with all of these racing thoughts and calls to the makeup lady, *sheitel* lady, caterer, band, and of course make time for my *chasan* and get him to think that I have my act together?

Now, let me go through the response cards, phone messages, and texts. With today's technology, people respond in a variety of ways and the caterer is pressuring me for an exact head count. Some people have written heartfelt messages. I wish I had the presence of mind to respond in kind, but I'm sure they understand.

Oh, look, here's a phone message from Yocheved — she's coming! I wish I could have a nice chat with her instead of all the other "to-dos" on the list. Yet I know what happens when I call her…a few minutes so easily turns into an hour, which I just can't spare right at the moment. At least I'll text her and let her know how excited I am to have her there at my *simchah*. "Dear Yocheved, can't wait to see you!" If anyone understands busy, it's Yocheved. And she's certainly not one to bear a grudge.

Let's see; is it possible I'm forgetting any details? Luckily, this isn't a Cleveland wedding. There, the protocol is to organize transportation for all of the out-of-town guests, but here there are so many weddings, that would be just impossible. I don't know people in this community yet, and it's too soon to ask my *chasan* to impose on his family when that isn't done in this community. Yocheved hasn't said a word yet; she probably understands and has no such expectations. Oh, look who's calling; it's Yocheved! "Hi, how are you? So excited you'll be sharing the big day with me. I miss you.

"You're wondering about transportation. Oh, funny you should ask. It's not done here in this community, so if you want, I'll split the car service if it's difficult for you." Although wedding expenses are mounting, I felt I had to offer something. I wish I could pick her up, but I guess on my wedding day there are some other commitments. I'm sure Yocheved will understand. She's the greatest!

■ ■ ■

MAZAL TOV, I'M MARRIED TO a wonderful guy. A second chance for happiness. Thank You, Hashem, for bringing me to this point.

"Betzalel, I'm looking forward to showing you around Cleveland. You wouldn't believe the out-of-town mentality. They wait on you hand and foot. I actually kind of miss that lifestyle. I can just call friends and ask them to do an airport run and it's a non-issue. A person like Yocheved has always been there for me, and would drop everything to do this kindness. I'll call her right now." I pulled out my phone, excited to talk to my friend. I've been so busy setting up my home and making my children comfortable that I have no time for a social life.

"Hi, Yocheved, long time, no speak! What does your schedule look like on Sunday? How would you like the privilege of bringing me and my wonderful new husband to the airport?"

27

ON CALL

Nervous Mom Speaks:

As an experienced mother of a large family, I don't usually panic or run to the doctor when my children get sick. Most often the virus will run its course, and TLC is usually the best prescription I can offer. However, the other night, when my daughter's feet swelled to twice their normal size in addition to the raised red splotches all over her normally creamy skin, I'll admit it; I panicked. Do these things ever happen at convenient times? It was 10:30 p.m., and I debated whom to call: the *frum* GP who is kind, warm, and lives around the corner, or the *frum* pediatrician who's a little more official. I voted for option one.

"Sounds like an allergic reaction," the GP said. "Tylenol, Benadryl, and she should be fine. But just in case I'm wrong, since I don't deal with childhood ailments, give your pediatrician a call. If he says anything different, will you call me and let me know?"

Thanking him warmly for his advice and feeling mildly relieved, I picked up the phone and dialed Shira, our pediatrician's wife, who happens to be a friend of mine. We go to the same gym and our kids play together on a regular basis. My heart continued to hammer nervously, especially when I stole another peek at Shiffy's feet, and I looked forward to hearing Shira's soothing voice.

"Hi, Shira, how are you?" I began.

"Hi," she replied.

"Is your husband available, by any chance?" I squeaked, fighting to squelch my panic that was rising again.

"Is this a medical question?" Her tone suddenly sounded aloof and business-like.

"Yes," I said, waiting for her to pass the phone to her husband.

"He prefers to be called on his pager," she said coldly.

"Ah," I said. "I understand." I got it; really, I did. Boundaries are good, especially when there are people around who can and will easily take advantage. But considering that I'm not one of these types and I can't remember ever calling Dr. Rofatsky at home, I'd assumed she would let me duck under the rope of officialdom, and pass on my call to the good doctor.

"Can you give me that number, please?"

"People are supposed to call the office," she replied, and my blood began to boil. *Are we friends or not? Have I ever called you like this? Can't you realize that I'm really nervous and just give me the number?*

"If you can give me the number now, I'll remember to call

the office in the future if I need to," I replied, stunned by her attitude.

With a loud sigh she acquiesced, and I paged her husband. When he called back and I described my daughter's condition, condescension dripped from his voice when he asked, "Have you tried Benadryl?" This was in stark contrast to the GP, whose warmth and caring had radiated from his voice, reassuring me that my question was valid and that he was there to help, professionally and as a friend.

Thanking him, I ended our call, and stoked the embers of my fury. *How dare she! And I thought we were friends!* How many countless times have people called me with their questions, asking me to "do them a favor" and check with my husband. As the vice principal of a day school, he is in high demand. Occasionally I, too, direct them to his school office; for non-urgent matters he also doesn't appreciate handling calls from home. But I do my utmost to portray kindness and concern, never a curt, cold attitude. I know, I know, I can't apply the way I do *chesed* to someone else. Surely Shira Rofatsky does plenty of her own *chasadim*, and this is simply an area where she and her husband jointly decided that a firm hand is required. They probably got burned one time too many before initiating this policy. But I still maintain that one must know with whom she is dealing. Considering the fact that I have never done this before and therefore must really be consumed by worry to breach the normal protocol, I'd have at least appreciated a pleasant response.

When I next saw Shira, I found myself unable to let go and treat her with my normal easygoing manner. I suppose I need some time. Maybe I even woke her up. Who knows? Grrr…

Shira Speaks:

"This just can't continue," I told my husband. "Of course, your devotion is admirable. The whole community values you and needs you. Yet lately the kids and I don't have a husband or father. We have Dr. B. on call always, attached to your pager. We miss you and need to know that we have a priority space with you. When was the last time we had a meaningful conversation that wasn't interrupted by a mother nervous about her child's condition?" This isn't the first time we've had this conversation, but it seems that my husband is more open to hearing my perspective.

"Shira, I hear you and know that *chesed* begins at home. I haven't learned or played with our boys for the longest time. When we got married, you and I dreamed of providing an oasis for anyone in need, to have that open door and be ready to help. But I agree; it's gone too far, and it's detracting from our family, our first priority. I'd love to have time off from being Dr. B. and just be your husband and the father of our children."

"This will be difficult to achieve because we've created expectations in our community," I said. "No one thinks twice before calling us at any time of day or night."

How will we be able to change this? My husband needs time off. He looks tired, and is nodding in agreement that something needs to change.

"It's true, and changing those practices is going to require a special plan that we stick to with total commitment. Shira, I'm ready when you are, but trust me, this will be very difficult for both of us. It will require setting strict boundaries and enforcing them consistently without exception in the beginning. Once the expectation is no longer there, we'll be free to make occasional exceptions for really desperate situations. However, let's think about this logically. A parent with a sick child after hours has the option to go to an urgent care center, a hospital, or call the pager for whichever doctor is on call at that time. A doctor has the right to have a life after work and his family has the right to his time and attention."

This conversation gives me hope, yet both of us are such softies. Perhaps we have to expect obstacles and create a plan that helps us to overcome them.

Okay, let's brainstorm some potential obstacles:

- ⇨ Nervous first-time mothers who are literally panicking
- ⇨ Parents who assure you it is only a quick question
- ⇨ Parents who have a friendly relationship with us so they feel free to expect the extra mile

Wow. This is eye-opening. If these are the obstacles we envision after only a couple of minutes of thinking, certainly there must be many others lurking. Clearly, if we have a different policy for each obstacle, people will feel hurt and confused. Our community is small and some will say that they can call us at home and there is no problem, while others will feel rejected.

"Shira, this will be hard for you," my husband said, "you're so warm and giving. But we both know there's only one way to restore our family life. We need to have a clear, no-exceptions policy to separate home from work. No matter who calls, they must be asked politely to call my pager and then I can take care of it accordingly. Some of our friends and neighbors may get upset. But our family is more important. And everyone will get used to it, eventually."

"Yes, you're right. I know it will be tough, yet our family needs this. This plan is a life preserver in turbulent waters."

He smiled at me, "It already helps to know that we share the same values and that this evolved because we both want to do good."

I felt a buzzing in my pocket, "Interestingly enough, my cell is ringing. Oh, it's only my friend, though it may be my very first challenge… Hi, how are you? Oh, you want to speak to my husband?" My mood soured quickly.

I thought, "Why did my first challenge have to be a friend who doesn't ordinarily call? We made a deal and consistency in all situations is an integral part of success. I must be firm and clear. I didn't realize how painfully difficult this would be. It's almost as if I need to turn off my natural switch for compassion. Maybe…no, I must keep affirming: compassion to family first. Okay, think of the greater good, and that people do have a host of other options. And remember, the first time will be the hardest. I have to just be a tape recorder playing a businesswoman. I can do this."

I took a breath to steel my nerves. "Yes, I'm sorry, but my husband prefers to receive all medical calls through his business. Thank you for your understanding and have a pleasant evening."

28

RULING MY ROOST

Chani Speaks:

"Good night, sweetie," I said, bending down to plant a kiss on little Avrami's cheek. "Sleep well."

Closing his door halfway, I breathed a sigh of relief. Phew! Avrami and Shiffy are down, baby's quiet, so now I could hand the kids over to Reuven and run to Rebbetzin Melamed's parenting class. She always has so much to give over. I wondered what her topic would be this time.

The class seemed to fly by in minutes, even though it was over an hour long. Wow, what a class! It was really up my alley, too.

Rebbetzin Melamed stressed the importance of structure and orderliness in children's lives, reiterating how they should have a schedule for mealtimes, school work, bedtime, and really for just about everything that happens during their day. She says this will help them become organized adults who can function effectively in the real world. Equally important, she said, is for them to take care of their belongings and have a set place where they keep each of their things.

"Have you ever seen," the Rebbetzin asked, a small smile playing on her lips, "the mother who's trying to herd her brood out the door, and little Mindy suddenly appears wearing her jacket but no shoes? The mother's face turns red, and she gets flustered, repeatedly glancing at her watch as her tension grows. 'We're going to be late!' she announces, her words sounding like staccato notes. Her tension increases as the frantic search for shoes ensues…"

Chuckles filled the room as the ladies nodded knowingly. It seemed like a familiar picture to many. But I straightened my shoulders and determined that this would never resemble the portrait of my home. I'll rule my roost; my roost won't rule me.

Armed with determination to transform my basically organized home into tip-top shape, I began writing lists as soon as I got home. My children will learn to value the importance of time and organization.

"Okay, kids," I told Shiffy and Avrami the next afternoon, "line up all of your riding toys under the stairwell. Then you can come up and eat lunch."

"But, Ma," Shiffy protested. "It takes so much longer to get them out if we put them over there. Can't we just leave them out?"

"Absolutely not," I retorted, working hard to keep my voice calm while my insides churned. Will Shiffy be my black sheep? I hope she won't be the one who can't find her missing shoe just when it's time to go, making the whole family late for school. Or her homework, or her lunch…what a disaster! I shuddered and squared my shoulders. *Not if I can help it*, I determined.

"No lunch until every toy is put in its place," I reiterated firmly, priding myself on staying resolute and maintaining my standards.

"Can you read me a story?" Avrami pulled on my skirt a little later, holding his favorite book, *The Royal Mission*.

I checked my watch and then my list.

"No *zeeskeit*, I'm sorry," I told him, patting his shoulder. "I have to start making dinner now so it can be ready on time."

Because if dinner is served late, baths will be late, bedtime will run later, and we may all oversleep the next day, and what a disaster that would be! Not to mention the fact that everyone will be moody and *kvetchy* all day.

Turning toward the stove to begin making dinner, I caught the sad slump of Avrami's shoulders as he shuffled away. *He'll be grateful when he's old enough to understand*, I assured myself, deftly dicing some vegetables and tossing them into the frying pan.

The week flew by with my solid attempts of keeping order every step of the way. I wondered what Rebbetzin Melamed would speak about this time.

I quickly and efficiently served dinner and was working hard on the bedtime routine so I could attend another fabulous lecture. Suddenly, a knock sounded on my door.

"Hi, Chani." It was my neighbor, Tova. "Can I borrow an onion?"

Masking my disapproval, I pasted a smile on my face and went to get her the onion. If she had made a proper shopping list, I was sure she wouldn't have needed to borrow such a staple. And anyway, why is she just starting to cook dinner now?

"Here you go," I said, handing it over as I closed my door.

Yikes! I'm five minutes behind because of the onion interruption.

What will the others think if I show up late for the class?

"Avrami, out of the bath already! It's Shiffy's turn!" I yelled.

"But I'm playing," he protested, making honking noises as he steered his boat around the bathtub.

Having his best interest in mind, I yanked the boat out of his hand and flipped the lever, letting the water swish down the drain.

"Bath time is over, darling. We have to get you to bed."

Carrying a howling, towel-clad Avrami, I promptly began putting on his pajamas. If I tried really hard, I should still be able to make it on time.

Slightly out of breath, I made it! *So there wasn't time for bedtime stories tonight*, I mused, sliding into my seat. *But I know I'll come back recharged after culling some new wisdom on how to run my home in the best possible way. What better gift can I give my family?*

Fabulous, just amazing, I thought, coming home and opening the door to my complex. As I walked in, I tripped, finding my balance in the nick of time. *That was close*, I thought, clutching the banister and breathing hard. But what was that? I stared in horror as I realized exactly what *it* was. Why, Tova's kids had left all of their riding toys all over the place! Where exactly did that leave a path for us to walk? Didn't she ever hear the words "order" and "organization"? Apparently not! I'll call her immediately and tell her that it's simply not acceptable to have such a lackadaisical attitude. Even if she's not worried about her children's future, she still has to prioritize the safety of the other residents in our building!

Marching up the stairs and planning exactly what I'd tell her, I passed by her apartment and heard children's voices. *What in the world are they doing up at this hour?* I wondered, horrified. This situation was going from bad to worse. After I tell her my piece, maybe I'll invite her to join me for Rebbetzin Melamed's next lecture. She can really use the help…

Tova Speaks:

My garbage can overflows with crumpled up notes of words unspoken to my neighbor, Chani. The emotional intensity reminiscent of high school allowed the escape of a small smile, quickly masked by the angst of feeling judged and misunderstood. Ever friendly and optimistic Tova, they called me, the girl who never needed an umbrella because it just wouldn't rain, although I did get drenched at times. The girl who was elected peacemaker because of a severe allergy to conflict of any kind is dreaming of relocating to her own house away from the hustle and bustle of apartment life. What is happening in my internal world?

I'm a young girl again and dreading Sundays because my sister and I had to clean the whole house before we were allowed to make any social arrangements. My sister seemed to actually enjoy the chores, while the mop and vacuum taunted me and kept me away from playing with my friends. I promised myself that my children wouldn't grow up with that experience, and so they don't.

Yet, somehow I wound up in an apartment building with a very militant neighbor who wants to control our public living area. I'm happy to let my darling children leave their bikes parked on a slant and enjoy the carefree time of being children. Of course, I enjoy the rare occasion when my house is neat. Yet, there are priorities. I choose nurturing my children over rigid structure that doesn't allow them the wings to fly. They revel in my love and there is no tension in their cute, little pudgy shoulders as they race around on their riding toys, singing at top volume. Our bedtime hour is from seven to eleven, and each child gets a private conversation about his day and his feelings. And we don't have pantry locks so that my children can have a full kinesthetic experience with each texture. When they experiment cleaning up the confectionary sugar on the kitchen counter with water, well, the icing can rival the best recipes in any cookbook and the camera captures their antics for posterity. My apartment wouldn't win an award in a good housekeeping periodical, but the sounds of laughter echoing out of it bring a smile to many faces.

Chani seems to believe that she must teach me how to educate my children. When I came home from the park yesterday with a long list of phone calls to make, she greeted me with a smile and a mop; yes, that old instrument of torture. She suggested that we clean the common areas together and stack up the toys in a perfect line by five every afternoon so that dinner can follow, and then baths and bedtime, like clockwork.

If she wants to raise toy soldiers all in a row, that is her prerogative. I see the yearning in her children's eyes when they see my children playing gleefully in the sand, unrestrained by warnings of stains or time alerts every five minutes.

The last thing I want is confrontation with Chani, yet her insistence on one approach is triggering intense emotion, and yes, on a deeper level, feelings of inadequacy. I never could keep things tidy like my sister. Somehow, mess challenged me. There were always so many more enjoyable activities that beckoned to me and tempted me to procrastinate those tasks I found distasteful and utterly nonstimulating. And besides, how can Chani be so sure that when raising young children, total adherence to tidiness doesn't cramp their style?

Maybe I should call the parenting expert, Mrs. Melamed, and give her a bit of information so that Chani and her children can receive the guidance that they need. Why should I have to run away when I'm not imposing my style on anyone? Now, that's a good idea.

Ever optimistic Tova is making a comeback.

"Hello, Mrs. Melamed, it's Tova. I need your help with a situation in my apartment building."

29

IT'S A MATTER OF "PRINCIPAL"

Mother Speaks:

"Ma?" Estie blew in with a bang, and I winced as the door slammed, giving the house a good shake. "I just found out that they're dividing our class next year! Some girls will get Mrs. Diamond, and the others will have this brand-new teacher. I think this might be her first year teaching — ever." Estie's eyes were wide with incredulity. "Can you call Mrs. Oved and make sure I get Mrs. Diamond, please?"

"Let me think about this a little," I said, turning back to stir the mushroom-barley soup simmering on the stove. "Of course I want to help you. I just don't want to do anything hasty."

"But, Ma," Estie begged, coming beside me. "Everyone always has a fabulous year with Mrs. Diamond. She's an amazing teacher. Besides, all the mothers are calling and requesting Mrs. Diamond. So all of my friends will be in that class. Please, Ma?"

"I'll see what I can do," I assured my anxious daughter, and my thoughts started whirling. "Just give me a few minutes to think please, okay?"

I'm not the complaining type, and I really like to save my calls to the principal for something really urgent so she takes me seriously. Also, I don't like to bother busy people for minor issues, especially someone like Mrs. Oved. Everyone knows how much time she puts into her work, and that when the school day ends, the light in her office continues burning for hours. And many people don't seem to have boundaries. I have plenty of friends and acquaintances who don't hesitate to call her at home for all sorts of matters, disregarding the fact that she's human and may just want to have a life outside of school. I seriously wonder who has a more consuming job, a doctor or a principal. I guess being a mother is pretty consuming, too, but there are occasional quiet interludes… Uh-oh, are Shimmy and Tova at it again? What was I thinking? Phew. The battle ended without my intervention. Deep breath and back to the situation.

The question is if this matter is urgent enough to warrant a call to the principal. Let's weigh the issues. Having a year under the tutelage of a veteran, tried-and-true educator vs. experiencing a novice and being a guinea pig. Hmm… Being in a class with all of her friends or being in the other class with girls that aren't really her type… Double hmm… I wouldn't be surprised, knowing Estie's class, if they divide the class according to levels. Mrs. Oved will probably assign the lower level class to the new teacher. As a veteran,

Mrs. Diamond will probably want to teach the more advanced students, and I'm sure she'll get her preference. Academically, Estie falls right in the middle, so there's a good chance that they might place her with this new, inexperienced teacher.

I wrinkled my eyebrows and sent up a quick *tefillah* for *siyata d'Shmaya*. And then I knew in a burst of stunning clarity what I needed to do. What took me so long to reach that conclusion?

Yes, I think a phone call is definitely warranted. After all, an entire year of Estie's *chinuch* is at stake. And we all know that each year is a building block. If she has a bad experience this year, it could turn her off to learning for the rest of her school career! This is definitely a time to pick up the phone and fight for my daughter's rights. Putting on my mother-bear armor, I prepared to take up the cause.

Marching into my bedroom for privacy, I picked up the phone, determined not to take no for an answer.

"Bais Leah, may I help you?"

"May I speak with Mrs. Oved, please?"

Mrs. Oved Speaks:

What was I thinking when I accepted a position as principal? Or perhaps an even better question may be the same question that I like to put to certain students: Was I thinking?

Yes, as the violins softly played, I dreamed of making an impact on the next generation of fertile minds and hearts, guiding teachers, helping parents, and inspiring a cohesive environment where each member of the team shares the same vision…

Yet I didn't begin to realize the politics involved in seemingly simple technical tasks such as class placement. Theoretically, a principal receives reports from each teacher about the academic, social, and emotional development of each student, including how the student is doing individually and within the context of her group. Based on that information and her personal knowledge of each student's history, the principal chooses the teacher's style that would be the best fit for continued success in addition to the healthiest group dynamic simultaneously.

To add to the complexity of this jigsaw puzzle, the principal must also weigh the benefits and risks of creating leveled classes, louder groups or quieter groups, groups from the same neighborhood, or groups from similar backgrounds... She must work to avoid elitism, yet still achieve a cohesive learning environment.

No matter how many cups of coffee later, each piece of the jigsaw that finds a spot triggers a question of another placement. As you may have noticed, this taxing summer job isn't the favorite of this principal or any of my colleagues, who are no doubt nodding their heads and smiling in recognition of this challenge. If it ended there, it would still be mission close to impossible, yet that is only the beginning. Now, passionate parents enter the zone believing in advocating for their children and convinced that they know which teachers hold the keys to their children's success and future and which ones may deprive their children of achieving their potential. Respectful of their advocacy, yet unable to divulge that the very friend they believe to be a necessary ingredient for their children's health is the very friend whose parents requested a change because they think the relationship is unhealthy. Countless examples that involve confidential reasons for teacher selection and social preferences hit the principal's desk via e-mail, sealed envelopes, and phone calls.

Speaking of which, the mother on the phone is a passionate advocate for her child.

"Hello, how are you? And, how is our Estie?

"You do understand that I can't divulge yet which class your daughter will be in next year. You have been a loyal parent here for years. I admire that you want to ensure the best possible educational experience for your daughter. That is my hope for every student in this school.

"Please understand that there are so many considerations that I'm not at liberty to share, which play a role in determining the best fit. And those include balancing the needs of every student and matching them with the best fit, keeping all the academic, social, spiritual, and learning styles in mind. It's like a Rubik's Cube in that when you solve one side, there's another puzzle that surfaces on the other side. Allow me to reassure you that my door is always open to you and that sometimes when we look back we see that what our child learned was actually exactly what she needed that year, even though it's not always in synchrony with our initial perspective.

"I'll be glad to take your thoughts and opinions into serious consideration. We are a team. But I do need your trust that I have the utmost concern for the needs of every child in this school. They are all my children. I wake up thinking about them, go to sleep thinking about them, and work with them in the interim."

As the conversation continued, the truth came out. It wasn't the mother's idea to make this phone call; indeed, her daughter had initiated this phone conference.

"You do know that we don't take elementary student requests for teachers. I'm confident that an experienced mother, such as yourself, knows how to help her reframe if that proves to be necessary. And just to let you know, our new teacher, Miss Sugarman, has excellent qualifications. I understand your reservations, however, contrary to what your daughter heard, this is not Miss Sugarman's first year teaching. She has a reputation for making a lasting impact on her students. Thank you for your interest and your phone call."

No one warned me how painfully hard every call like this would be and what a toll it takes. My mind knows I can't please everyone and that I can't make decisions based on which parent's plea was expressed most eloquently, but my heart sings a different melody. A parent who takes an active interest in her child's education is an asset. How many parents have told me that I should just take care of the education and they'll get the teeth brushed? That's definitely not the partnership of my dreams.

Yet there's another side of me bristling. Don't these parents have any trust in their school administration? Why isn't anyone willing to give Miss Sugarman a chance? If I still had a school-age child, I would definitely entrust her to Miss Sugarman's care. I think…

The coffee in the staff room smells especially aromatic today. And perhaps it will help to heal the pounding headache that seems to follow phone calls of this nature.

30

READING BETWEEN THE LINES

Chani Speaks:

Nestled in a small corner plaza centrally located in the Jewish community of Rolling Hills, Sifriyah was the place to pick up Jewish books and other assorted Judaica items. Owned and managed by the Mekovskys, the little store had been a fixture in town for almost as long as Chani could remember. When the Mekovskys first showed up in the neighborhood, Chani felt charmed by their sweet mannerisms and wanted to help this immigrant family succeed. Her heart ached for all of the difficulties they would encounter as Russians trying to merge into the big American melting pot, and she felt driven to ease their plight. Hadn't they suffered enough in Russia? And who knew what one Jew could do when she set her mind to it? Perhaps she could even encourage their interest in Yiddishkeit.

When she invited them for that first Shabbos meal a lifetime ago, they told her they were both doctors in Russia but couldn't practice in the US without going back to school.

"But we have to pay the bills," they said in thick accents. "We don't have money."

For the next few weeks the Mekovskys embedded themselves in Chani's mind. She felt driven to help them, but couldn't figure out what to do to ease their transition. Until she stopped by their home one *erev Shabbos* to deliver a cake and got the answer she was looking for.

A collection of old Jewish books lined one wall of their modest living room. And spread throughout the room Chani noticed some beautiful, old Judaica items. There was a large silver menorah, several silver Kiddush cups of assorted styles and sizes, and a three-tier silver Seder plate.

And suddenly, Chani had a brainstorm.

"You know what Rolling Hills needs?" Chani exclaimed. "A Judaica store would fill such a void here! It's the perfect thing, and I think you'd be amazingly successful! I know you will!"

On the wings of prayer and with tremendous effort, Sifriyah was born. Mrs. Mekovsky always had a cheerful greeting for all of her clientele. But lately, Chani had noticed a worried frown sitting on Mrs. Mekovsky's lips, and when she popped into Sifriyah from time to time, it was impossible to ignore the glaring void of customers. Opening Sifriyah's glass door one afternoon, a loud silence enveloped her, and her heart constricted.

"How are you, Mrs. Mekovsky?" Chani ventured to the older

Russian lady, hoping to see the trademark smile on her lips.

A loud sigh answered her question.

"Business isn't so good," Mrs. Mekovsky confided. "I'm wondering if we will have to close our doors."

Chani gasped and put a hand over her mouth.

"But we need you!" she protested. "Rolling Hills wouldn't be the same without you!"

A pile of guilt settled on Chani's shoulders as her well-meaning advice from way back resounded in her mind. *Was this her fault? Had she led this sweet, innocent family down the wrong path?*

"Ach!" Mrs. Mekovsky waved a tired hand, as if brushing away Chani's protests. "These days everyone gets what they need online. It's easier, just a click of a button and poof! It comes straight to their house. When we first emigrated many years ago, we filled a need. But now, maybe it's time to face the facts; we aren't wanted anymore."

Chani swallowed over a hard lump in her throat. This was terrible! With courage and determination, they had built up a small family business, and concurrent with its growth was their stepping up the ladder in commitment to Yiddishkeit. And now, would they be forced to begin anew again? And at this point, in their older years? Where was the loyalty owed to them?

"It's probably just a dry spell," Chani soothed, wanting to wipe the pain from Mrs. Mekovsky's chocolate eyes. "You'll see."

"No," Mrs. Mekovsky said in a hard, disappointed tone. "It's been like this for a long time already. Right before a Yom Tov the store is busy. But in between?" With a sweep of her arm, she gestured to the empty store. "It's like this."

While Chani browsed the shelves in search of a new book, her mind wandered.

Why would people be so disloyal? Don't they see the obligation to support local Yidden? I just don't understand it. Not overly computer savvy, Chani couldn't relate to the pull of Internet shopping. *What's so difficult about a five-minute drive?* She shook her head, pronouncing judgment on her community. *It's just not right,* she thought, shaking her head with frustration.

"Have a good day, Mrs. Mekovsky," Chani wished her. "I hope things pick up."

Mrs. Mekovsky flashed a small smile, but it didn't reach her eyes.

Later that afternoon, Chani's daughter, Dini, came home from school bursting with excitement.

"Ma, there's this amazing new Jewish game out I'd really love to get before our Shabbaton! Everyone's talking about it. But my friends told me you can only order it online. Can we use your work computer and order it? Please? Please?"

"Are you sure Sifriyah doesn't have it?" Chani asked, seeing Mrs. Mekovsky's woebegone expression in her mind's eye.

"They for sure won't have it! And by the time they order it and get it in, it would be too late, I'd never have it in time. Please, Ma? Can I show you the website?"

Leading Dini into the study, Chani watched as her daughter deftly pushed buttons and a Jewish website sprang up in seconds.

"See?" Dini bubbled, "It's only fifteen dollars, and there's even free shipping if you order today. Okay, Ma?"

Giving her the green light, Dini ordered the game and left the study humming happily.

That really was quick and easy, Chani mused, sautéing some vegetables to go with supper. *Ohmigoodness! Ahuva's birthday is next week, and I didn't get her a gift yet!* Ahuva was turning nineteen and attending her second year of seminary in Baltimore. *Hey! Maybe I can order a book online and get it shipped!*

Chani, she chided herself as she poured spices on the chicken.

What happened to loyalty? Sifriyah, remember? Go over there, pick out a book, run to the post office... Chani sighed. *But I have so much to do this week. What harm can there be if I just peek and see if I find anything?* And while supper was cooking, Chani opened her browser, found a brand-new historical novel that was just Ahuva's type, and in a manner of minutes, the purchase, shipping, and handling were all wrapped up.

A pang of guilt pierced her heart. *Did I just do something wrong? Now that I see how easy it is, I can understand the inclination to do my shopping this way. Does that make me guilty of disloyalty, also? Will I bear responsibility along with the community if Sifriyah has to close its doors? No*, Chani told herself firmly. *This is just a one-time aberration. If they go out of business, it will have nothing to do with me.*

A few days later Chani passed her calendar and noticed she had a bar mitzvah to attend the following Tuesday evening. *Good thing I looked; I totally forgot about it!* Relief quickly changed to discomfort. *I never got a gift. How can I show up without a gift?* There was absolutely no way she would have time to run to Sifriyah during the next few days. She was backlogged at work, even putting in overtime, and from the moment she got home, she would be steamrolled quickly through supper, homework, and bedtime, occasionally finding time to take a few breaths.

What should I do? And then it came to her: JudaicaGems.org, the place for all your Judaica needs. *Maybe just this once*, Chani told herself. *After all, this is an extenuating circumstance, and they'll have it shipped to me in two days.*

That Tuesday evening, Chani and her husband entered the hall and placed their gift on the large table brimming with colorfully wrapped presents.

"Hello, Chani."

"Mrs. Mekovsky, how are you?"

"Baruch Hashem, Chani. And you?"

Ohmigoodness, she knows! She saw me put down a gift, and she knows I didn't get it from Sifriyah! Oh, why did I have to run into her now? Should I explain? Not say anything? Beg for her understanding and tell her this was a one-time deviation, reassuring her that I'm staunchly loyal through and through?

As Chani was embroiled in internal debate, she glanced at Mrs. Mekovsky, and what she saw made her flinch. The raw pain in her eyes was unmistakable, and Chani wished she could run for cover. Couldn't her cell phone ring or one of her friends come bounding out to extricate her from this mess?

Mrs. Mekovsky Speaks:

I wonder what is wrong with me lately. It's just one long sigh after another broken up by the occasional low moan. Life was so much harder in Russia. Everyone lived in constant fear of who might be an enemy. We didn't even know if our children would turn against us. The indoctrination of the Soviet educational system brainwashed many people against any other loyalty. Hard work was the lifestyle to earn even the barest minimum, yet one complaint never escaped my lips. Who would dare to utter a complaint in this Soviet paradise?

And then we came to America. Rest and relaxation were as much of a foreign language as English. Terms and concepts like vacation or leisure time couldn't enter my brain despite advanced educational degrees. I remember the first time being a guest at a Shabbos dinner where the family members actually laughed together. That was probably the turning point that propelled me to take a closer look at Yiddishkeit. People laughed comfortably and no one was scared or looked furtively behind them, and quickly pretended it was a coughing fit. I remember the first time our family laughed together; the sound was so different, I nearly called a doctor to make sure those sounds emanating from our throats weren't harmful. My husband, a very prominent doctor, reassured me — dangerous, no; contagious, yes!

Another sigh; America has made me a softie. Suddenly, hardship and pain are strangers. America gave us so many opportunities we didn't have in Russia. The taste of freedom is intoxicating. So many flavors, so many choices…

Then I think guiltily, *maybe Russia had a point*. What do people do with all these choices? They are bombarded with advertisements and competition that only distracts them… and then an old-fashioned bookstore practically loses its charm with its proximity to the endless possibilities winking at customers and casting their alluring spell.

I remember when the bookstore idea came up. My husband and I argued vehemently that the idea of Russian immigrants owning and managing a Judaica store is incongruous. How can we advise customers? We didn't count on Chani's persuasive talents and her confidence. She believed that my husband's desire to learn and make up for lost years coupled with his photographic memory would create a very inspirational brand for our community's bookstore. And initially she seemed right! Anyway, this musing is so American — let me clear my mind and enjoy the *simchah* tonight.

Maybe when the community sees me, they will remember their good old-fashioned homegrown bookstore. And I can always enjoy a nice chat with Chani. If there's anyone I totally trust, who doesn't get swept along with this tidal wave of everything at your fingertips with the touch of a button, it is she. I think I might pluck up the courage to speak to her about my feelings. Then I gaze at

Chani's pale face. *Chani, not you too!* The one person I thought had her life vest tightly fastened so as not to get swept away by the lure of instant…

"I was planning on speaking to you and sharing my real concerns and getting your advice. You helped us the first time. We might need new career guidance. I guess you resisted as long as possible."

"Wait, I can explain," Chani said, "it's not what it appears, it was a one-off. I'm loyal and do believe in supporting your efforts and the ideals of having a local bookstore."

"Chani, you don't understand. It's even harder now than before because we don't have the energy to begin all over again. I came to participate in this *simchah*, but just one glance at the gift table tells a story; a story of technology, a story of busy people who want all the convenience that only online can offer. And we simply can't compete with that nor am I sure we want to…"

"Mrs. Mekovsky, please listen," Chani pleaded.

"I listened to your assurances before and look where that got us. Forgive me, but I'll leave now. Maybe Russia had a point in teaching not to trust people because they will turn their backs on you when you have outgrown your usefulness to them. Chani, I thought you were the exception!"

Now that I'm home, I feel badly about my outburst to Chani. I was shocked, yet she did seem to genuinely care. Her eyes filled with tears when I told her I can't trust her. Can I allow myself to trust her? Maybe it's not black or white, Soviet or capitalist. Maybe there can be hope.

31

A WORK OF ART

Gitty Speaks:

Running nervous fingers through her wavy, auburn *sheitel*, Gitty took a deep breath and hoped that her artwork was at last satisfactory. She had worked long and hard on the cover jacket for Moshe Beller's new book and lost track of the amount of changes they had attempted over the last few weeks. Communication whizzed through the air as she tried, time after time, to satisfy Moshe's grandiose vision while trying to maintain a presentation of dignity and subtlety. Looking at the computer screen, she breathed a sigh of relief and allowed herself a slight smile. *This one was good, really good.* She had a strong feeling that both her boss and Moshe would be satisfied, at last. The idea had flown into her mind late last night, robbing her of much needed sleep, and at four in the morning, she finally tossed her comforter aside and slid into her computer chair. And now, finally, just as the first hues of sunrise streaked the sky, her design was born. It was an amazing thing, really, to see a picture in your mind take physical form and shape and become reality.

Time for a break, Gitty decided, noting the time. There was time for at least one cup of coffee before six-month-old Shaina and two-year-old Motti would awaken and demand their due.

Sitting at the oval kitchen table overlooking her deck, Gitty relaxed and checked in with her best friend. "Hi, Chaya, how are you?"

"Baruch Hashem, I hope. Too early to tell. I'm starting my diet today, and I'm already hungry. On another note, Gitty, I wanted to let you know that *HaOlam's* graphic designer is leaving. I already put in a good word for you to my boss. Wouldn't that be amazing if we could be coworkers?"

"Interesting," Gitty replied haltingly. "I mean it would be fabulous, actually. I'd have to see what's involved."

"Well, of course," Chaya said. "But don't be surprised if you get an email or a phone call from Dovid Fuchs about the position. I really hope you get it."

"Thanks, Chaya," Gitty said. "You're a real friend."

A new job? She had been working for Amukah Publications for five years, ever since graduating seminary. The hours were convenient; she was able to send the children off in the morning and pick them up by three, and the pay, while she would love to see an increase (who wouldn't?), was satisfactory. She knew her way around Amukah, had friends and pleasant relationships with coworkers, and enjoyed a respectful relationship with her boss. If she were offered a new job with HaOlam, a much more prestigious company, would she, should she, take it?

Let's not get ahead of yourself, she cautioned herself. *After all, you haven't even gotten an offer yet. For all you know, there's a mile-long list of potential graphic artists who have much more impressive qualifications.*

Quickly closing the window on her musings, she downed the last drops of her coffee just as Shaina and Motti began to harmonize their wakeup calls.

The email wasn't long in coming. During a mid-morning break, Gitty's heart began beating rapidly as she grazed over the note from *HaOlam*.

> Dear Mrs. Bloom,
>   *HaOlam* is seeking a talented graphic artist to fill a recently vacated position. Your work comes highly recommended, and I wondered if we could set up a time to meet and discuss possible employment.
>   Looking forward to hearing from you,
>   Dovid Fuchs
>   Executive Editor, *HaOlam* Weekly Magazine

Well, there's certainly no harm in meeting, Gitty decided, rapidly sending a note in return.

Several days later, Gitty wandered around in a fog. *HaOlam* had offered her a position that required only two hours more a day than her current job, but the salary was significantly higher. Their system was much more high-tech than what Gitty was used to; it would be like learning a whole new language. Was she up to that challenge? Should she trade in her veteran status in her current job, where people respected her abilities, for a job where she would begin as a novice, having to learn everything from scratch?

The possibility was intriguing. On the other hand, her Bubby always used to say, "If it's not broken, why fix it?"

On the other hand (she was grateful that she only had two hands), if Hashem was gently depositing this position in her lap, perhaps it was foolish to say no. Certainly, as the kids got older and perhaps more joined the fray, a larger income would be helpful, even necessary. Maybe the extra influx could help Yossi stay in *kollel* longer. And she was blessed with a wonderful babysitter who was almost part of the family. Bella would be only too happy to stay the extra hours, and the children would be content and well cared for. Shaking her head, she tried to dismiss her mother's disapproval of such a situation. After all, her mother had been a stay-at-home mom, firmly insisting that, "Children belong with their mama." As it was, her mother thought she was away for too many hours. Shuddering, she decided to cross that bridge if and when she came to it.

A *ping* in her inbox distracted her from her quandary.

"Gitty, the cover jacket is amazing! Outstanding work, *yasher kochacha*! Moshe Beller

Smiling, Gitty replied to the author's gratitude. And then a note from her boss quickly followed: "Knew you could bring it to life. Tuvia Fuchs

Wow! Talk about timing! Should she give up security, comfort, and a reputation? They were managing just fine on her salary now; why rock the boat? *But these opportunities don't come up all the time.* Perhaps if she didn't grasp it now, a time would come when they would need it and it wouldn't be available. *What to do?*

Picturing an Olympic-size pool, Gitty felt like she was poised, about to dive in. That first immersion was always an icy shock, but after that, her body would adjust, and the water would feel deliciously invigorating.

She could ask Yossi, but she knew he would toss the ball right back in her court, telling her this was her decision since it would mostly affect her.

And what about loyalty? Amukah had hired her fresh out of seminary, believing in her potential. No other agency would even glance at her at that early stage. Ever so patiently, they guided her to her current level of expertise. Was it fair to now transfer that expertise to a more prestigious company?

Chocolate, she decided. *It always helps me gain clarity, not to mention other things.*

Okay, here goes. I'm writing a list of pros and cons. I knew the chocolate would help me figure things out.

PROS:

1. Better salary

    a. To help Yossi stay in kollel

    b. Finance day-school tuitions when the time comes

    c. Save up for a house

2. Prestigious Company — good for reputation — nice addition to resume

3. Opening door to learning new skills and stepping up in my career

CONS:

1. More hours: will I be too tired to have patience for the kids? Will they miss me too much or be 'Mommy-deprived', even though they love Bella? Am I reneging on my most important career for the allure of some jingling coins and prestige?

2. Where is my loyalty to Amukah who planted me, watered me, and helped me grow?

> 3. Fear: what if I don't succeed in my new position? Am I relinquishing a secure job for an unknown where, if I fail I'll wind up with nothing?

I have to discuss this with Yossi, Gitty mused, in between creamy bites, *and beg him to give an honest opinion. But there is a convincing whisper pushing me to move onward and upward. After all, why were we put in This World if not to move forward? Hashem doesn't want us to remain robots, comfortably ensconced in the same place our whole lives, performing only tried-and-true tasks without reaching up to grasp new opportunities.*

I think, she mused, looking with regret at the empty wrapper, *I'm inclined to go for the gold. I might need more chocolate to face my boss after presenting my resignation. I wonder what diet Chaya's on… But Gitty, get a hold of yourself! You were just offered a job with a leading publishing company. You're going places, my friend, and it's wonderfully exciting. I can't wait to tell Yossi! Ready or not, HaOlam, here I come!*

The Boss Speaks:

Every now and again, there's is a genuine satisfying feeling when you take a risk, give a beginner a chance, and see the growth and development. I remember when we needed a graphic designer and there were so many applicants for the position. Many had experience and definite styles and undoubtedly could have done a beautiful job for our fledgling publishing company.

Yet, something about Gitty's innocence and hopeful eyes as she showed her impressive portfolio pulled at my heartstrings. Her youthful enthusiasm, refreshing openness to learning, and untainted creativity appealed as I considered all of the hopeful applicants and reviewed their credentials yet again. I understand the frustrations of every new graduate who receives rejections time after time since companies demand experience, and the old paradox surfaces that people need to be hired to get experience. I visualized the burned-out look of long-time job searchers and the feeling that their résumés get lost in deep black holes replacing Gitty's optimistic mindset. I can practically touch the decision process as if it were happening right this moment.

Now, I'm a businessman and I make decisions with my head, not with my heart, right? Just because she reminds me of my daughter doesn't mean I can't choose experience and a proven record over a new graduate, despite her promising qualities.

Time for a coffee. I'll buzz my secretary who makes an amazing brew exactly according to my tastes and never fails to stimulate my best thinking moments.

What are my primary goals here?

Getting Amukah Publishing on the map. Identifying a unique brand and flavor that people visualize when they think Amukah. Hiring a dedicated, enthusiastic, talented staff whose strengths complement each other. Choosing people who are able to be open to new ideas and willing to experiment.

It does appear that Gitty fills these requirements better than the other applicants and will probably be eternally grateful that I gave her this exciting opportunity. Fostering unity and employee satisfaction also belongs on my priority list.

What a trip into the past. And that was a phenomenal stroke of genius if I say so myself. Gitty outdoes herself with her creative work. The positive feedback pings constantly in my inbox and translates into better sales and more authors wanting to utilize our services. Sometimes, I wonder if she realizes how much her talents have blossomed. She truly has the capacity to work in a top-notch company. Wait a minute; we are top notch!

I know with complete certainty that Gitty is beyond grateful to us for our training and allowing her to grow in her own unique way. Funny, as I sit here musing, Gitty is knocking on the door. Come in, Gitty. What's wrong? You look a bit pale. You have been working hard. You know what, take a few days paid vacation together with your husband. My favorite designer deserves a bonus for her golden handiwork.

You want to talk with me. You have something to tell me. Gitty, you are leaving our company! You are submitting notice with the required thirty-day notification and moving on. You will always be grateful.

Well, I don't really know what to say. This comes as quite a shock and in my mind's eye, I pictured you as a fixture here at Amukah for many years. Is there something you were unhappy with regarding your work situation? Is there any way you might be willing to reconsider? I can't just simply accept this resignation without a proper conversation after all of these years of facilitating your rise to stardom. Please give me the courtesy of considering my request and go home, discuss this with your husband, and let's meet in three days. At that point, if this decision remains firm, I'll have no choice but to accept this with a heavy heart. After all, Amukah believes in employee satisfaction. Have a good afternoon, Gitty. I'll see you on Thursday at four.

32

A PIECE OF THE PIE

Gila Speaks:

After a long day at work followed by an even longer evening of supper and homework, my feet were aching and my head was spinning, and I was dreaming fluffy dreams of collapsing in bed with a good book. Just then the phone rang; it was my friend, Dalya. The last thing I wanted at that moment was a long phone call, but what could I do? *Chesed* isn't always convenient, and she seemed to really need to vent. So, postponing my wistful dreams, I thrust my arms into a sinkful of dishes, eyeing the clock nervously as the kids' bedtime ticked later and later. I listened, empathized, and *um-hmmed* often enough to show my interest and concern.

"They really won't give Yocheved her eighth grade diploma unless she brings up her math grade?" I was aghast. Yocheved was such a sweet girl. What would become of her if she couldn't go to high school together with her friends and peers? And suddenly, just as I picked up the last dirty glass, epiphany struck.

"Dalya!" I said, my voice brimming with excitement. "Why don't you send Yocheved to me a few times a week? I can help her with her math!"

"Oh, Gila," Dalya replied, and I could almost see her shaking wisps of her auburn *sheitel* out of her green eyes. "I can't ask you for that kind of favor. I wasn't calling to ask you for practical help; I just needed your ear, that's all. I mean, you work full-time, are juggling a family; how in the world would you have time for my daughter, too?"

"What are friends for?" I rejoined, setting the sparkling glass in the drainer and breathing a sigh of relief. "I'm a math teacher, after all, and I'd like to help. Send her to me a few times a week and she'll be up to snuff in no time, you'll see."

"Gila, you're a lifesaver," Dalya breathed. "But as much as I don't want Yocheved to be held back, I don't have money to pay you for tutoring a few times a week. I think the going rate is at least $50 an hour, and there's just no way we can do that. I wish we could, but we're always tight, you know that. With a large family, baruch Hashem, the needs are constant, and there never seems to be a month without some kind of major expense that sets us back yet again. People don't seem to eat out as much as they used to, either, so our pizza shop is struggling to stay afloat."

"Tell you what," I said, reaching for the broom and feeling very altruistic. "Talk with your husband and just pay me whatever you two think you can handle. Yocheved needs to graduate, and that's all there is to it. This is the perfect solution."

"I don't know what to say," Dalya replied. "You're amazing. I'll talk to Pinny and get back to you."

We settled on $10 a session, and sometimes it was even less. But it didn't bother me. I watched Yocheved grasp the concepts of pre-algebra that had been eluding her, and it was so rewarding. Her shy smile lit up her face when comprehension dawned, and I felt a deep bubble of satisfaction and accomplishment. She would graduate with her class where she belonged, and she would do so with confidence.

Our tutoring sessions continued for several months until finally Yocheved felt comfortable swimming alone.

"I'm so glad," I told her as we said good-bye at our last session. "But if you ever have any questions, just call me, I'm happy to help."

A few weeks later, I had *a day*. My phone rang very early in the morning; my very close friend was calling to tell me she'd just been diagnosed with a malignancy, and we cried together. Then, on the way to school, I got rear-ended and wound up waiting an hour until a police officer showed up to assess the damage and make a report. So I was late to work, the kids were late to school, and I was in quite a state, feeling like I was playing the main part in a scene that I hadn't auditioned for. My students, perhaps sensing my tenuous state of mind, were climbing the walls, acting unusually restless and chutzpadik. I found myself wishing the clock hands would move faster to bring this awful day to a close.

As I drove home, I tried to breathe deeply and decided it was time for some self-care. There was simply no way I was in any condition to make supper, clean up from supper, and plunge into a typical, hectic, breathless evening. I'll get dinner from Pinny's, I decided, pleased with my decision. We rarely indulge in such luxuries, but today was anything but a regular day. Surely Dalya and her husband would give us a discount, which would make it easier to handle this extra expenditure on our limited budget.

"Gila!" Dalya greeted me warmly, cheeks flushed from working behind the counter. "What a nice surprise! What can I do for you?"

"Hi," I said. "Good to see you, too! I've had a really hard day, so I decided a treat was in order. How about two pies, two orders of spicy fries, and a family salad?" I asked. *I'd love some soup and dessert, too. Should I? Or was I taking advantage? No, it's okay,* I told myself. *I gave her assistance when she was in need without a thought of reimbursement. For months. Now I'm the one in need. Life is a wheel — sometimes we give and sometimes we receive. And that's okay.*

"Um, can I add some of your famous onion soup and a dozen assorted cookies?"

"Of course." Dalya was busily punching numbers into the register. "That'll be $75, please."

Huh? $75?! Where was my discount, or even my free supper? After I tutored Yocheved for months, practically for free — this is my thanks? I don't get it!

Stymied, I fumbled for my credit card, while my emotions reached a hearty boil. *I'd never have ordered the extras had I known she would charge me full price. But it's not just the money, it's the principle. Where is her hakaras hatov? Maybe I should think twice before I offer my services the next time…*

Dalya Speaks:

It's so hard to be on the receiving end. I feel so very needy. We have a standing joke in our family that when my husband sings *Eishes Chayil* and praises her for the respectful way she interacts with her home staff, I'd also welcome the opportunity to be courteous to my cook, laundress, and cleaning help. All we need to do is hire them first. Minor details in life…

I remember when we used to play value games in high school and seminary, and I felt so righteous placing financial security on the bottom of my list. Financial security was just a value for materialistic people, not for the likes of me, thirsting for spiritual fulfillment. And yet, when my daughter needs a math tutor and I can't afford to pay appropriate value, I wonder: Is money only materialistic or will it help her to feel confident and master necessary skills? And when my children need new clothing or shoes and they feel deprived compared to most of their classmates, is that merely materialistic, or a healthy desire to live within the norms of their peer groups? Or yes, even when I just feel overwhelmed with the dual responsibilities of running our home and restaurant and can't afford the help that would ease the burden physically and emotionally, it seems to me that financial security isn't merely a vehicle for materialistic pleasure.

And then we face these very difficult conflicts. My dear friend Gila, who happens to be a math whiz, offered to tutor my daughter for almost nothing. She loves my daughter and she loves teaching and honestly doesn't need the money currently as her husband is doing very well financially. Gila agreed to take a minimal token just to make me feel like I'm paying and preserve my dignity. It's working beautifully, as she has bonded with my daughter, whose confidence with math has soared. Prior to this extra help, she was convinced she has a math disability and that she was hopeless, and now she realizes she's capable of understanding. I can't even place a value on confidence and optimism, not to mention rescuing her from the ultimate humiliation of being held back if she hadn't been able to get past this hurdle.

I have been busy thinking of how to express this gratitude, which transcends financial value. The easy way would be to invite Gila to a paid meal for her and her family in my restaurant. Yet that almost seems tit for tat, not to mention that it may even offend her. She clearly wanted to help my daughter while being extremely sensitive to our precarious financial situation. To give her a meal and cut out our profit in some way would undermine her efforts rather than honor them. It may be even trickier if she happens to show up, which she does occasionally, to charge her the regular price. Yet I know that at the end of the day, respecting a person's intentions and allowing them to give is also an act of giving. I have a different idea.

Every year, our shul seeks a worthy couple to honor, who truly personify the *middos* of kindness and generosity. I'm calling our rabbi today and sharing my nomination. Gila deserves far more than a meal, which is eaten and digested. She deserves recognition so the community can emulate her ways. I bet we can even organize a surprise video with her children speaking about what it was like to grow up in her home.

It has been a long time since I have felt so excited by an idea. Additionally, it reminds me that money is one way to give, but there are other ways that are perhaps even more meaningful.

You won't believe this, but here she comes, straight to purchase a meal. What a deserving honoree, always seeking ways to give while preserving her dignity. Although every fiber in me wants to say, "It's on the house," I'll allow her to give in accordance with what she truly wants to do.

"Hi, Gila. What would you like to order today?"

PART III

RECLAIMING OUR MISSING PEACE

*An outline of interventions
and sample interviews from our stories*

RECLAIMING OUR MISSING PEACE

By Mrs. Esther Gendelman MS, LPC, CPC
and Dr. Sharon Livingston, PhD

Based on ICARE: Internal Compassion
and Relationship Enhancement

There is no greater *berachah* than shalom, peace. The Torah is replete with examples of how highly Hashem values our interpersonal relationships. Only in a state of *achdus* can we achieve our potential as individuals and as a people. Yet the challenges can be daunting. We experience a wide range of emotional reactions in our interactions. Often, we wish that our anger, as well as the discomfort of other negative emotions, would conveniently vanish. Succumbing to anger doesn't make us feel very good about ourselves. Yet suppressing anger can backfire. It can lead to actual illness or expressions of hurt in overly intensive and inappropriate ways. Since Hashem created this wide array of emotions, they clearly have their time, place, and constructive use. We weren't designed to be stones in a static state, but are meant to grow and change through our life experiences.

How, then, can we achieve genuine *shalom* with other people?

Firstly, we need to recognize that the concept of not appeasing a person in the midst of anger applies to ourselves too.

We can only learn to accept the sacred endeavor of working toward *shalom* by first working through our emotions and owning them. It takes time to reach a calm and rational state where we can successfully navigate the turbulence, and forcing ourselves to do this prematurely will likely result in holding grudges or in self-deception.

In this calm state, we will then be ready to utilize the Torah tools of giving the benefit of the doubt and working to understand other people's mindsets.

The following questions are designed to take you through a path of honest reflection with the ultimate goal of achieving *shalom* by using your experiences to refine your *middos*.

If, *chas veshalom*, you are in any type of abusive relationship, please seek help. This questionnaire is only designed for the normal aches and pains that we experience just by virtue of our human imperfection.

Not every question will apply to every situation. We will provide a few examples from our book, in which we utilized this method successfully, to give you a taste of our recipe to work through emotions. We would love to hear your feedback and your own creative additions that work for you.

These questions are a great starting point for enhanced self-awareness, which is essential to growth. If you would like to learn more about yourself, consider working with a Torah-oriented relationship counselor. We wish you the joy and fulfillment of striving for *shalom* in your relationships.

ASSESSMENT

Take your temperature on a scale of 1–10.

10 is "I'm extremely agitated and upset" and 1 is "I'm cool as a cucumber." What number are you?

If your temperature registers as 6 or higher, realize that this isn't the time to discuss the situation with the other person. It's not even time to force yourself to figure out the issue. Instead, just allow yourself to feel what you are feeling and observe it with acceptance. Ironically, change can only occur after we accept our current situation.

Another way to understand this idea is to see this as a starting point to map out a path to your destination.

Take the time you need to cool down. There's a reason you are upset.

A deep breath can help, or a walk, or splashing some cool water on your face, or having a nice cool drink. Be very kind to yourself while trying to make sense of the situation.

When your temperature has come down to 5 or lower, it's possible to do further work.

How?

Step 1: Acknowledge that something is bothering you or upsetting you. You are human, and as humans we have a wide range of emotions and responses. Every emotion can be channeled productively and provide information that we can use to grow.

   a. What is it? What specifically is upsetting you?
   b. What did the other person do that triggered your feelings? Be specific.
   c. What impact did it have on you?
   d. What might it remind you of from your past?

Sometimes, it isn't the present event that's upsetting us but that it triggered something painful from our past. Recognizing that fact can help us in the present.

   a. What happened back then?
   b. How is this similar to what is upsetting you now?

The truth is that the only one you can change is yourself, no matter what is happening with the other person, no matter how disturbing their behaviors or intentions may have been.

Step 2: With that in mind, how (if at all) might you have contributed to the situation and the other person's actions?

Step 3: Ask Yourself: What would Hashem want from me now?

Step 4: What do I need to move in the direction of my ideal self?

Step 5: How might I access the part of me that is compassionate and caring?

Step 6: How might I transcend my immediate need to be right about this and not feel the need to win and blame?

Step 7: Reflect on a time where you successfully navigated a conflict. How did that happen? What allowed you to reconnect? What (if anything) might you borrow from that experience?

Step 8: What would you advise someone you love who approached you with the same dilemma? Give yourself the gift of love and friendship and advise yourself accordingly.

Step 9: After the incident, ask yourself, "Which part of this did I navigate well, and how might I do better in the future?"

WHAT'S THE BIG DEAL?

Interventions to help Blimi and Zalmy (pp. 51-55) understand one another and repair their hurt.

Blimi: Oh my goodness. I'm so upset!

Self counselor: Take your temperature, what is it?

Blimi: Oy. It's 11 on a scale of 1–10.

Self counselor: Okay, let's take a walk.

Blimi: Sounds good. I do need to walk this anger off.

[Half an hour later]

Blimi: [taking a deep breath] Okay, I think I can deal with this now.

Self counselor: Excellent! I'm so proud of you for taking a little time for yourself and cooling down enough to think about it. So what specifically was upsetting?

Blimi: My husband couldn't empathize with me. I was in so much pain, so upset. I was reaching out to him for some support and I didn't get any. Just like always!

Self counselor: Oh, that sounds awful. What did your husband do to trigger those feelings?

Blimi: He said, "No big deal!" It's so dismissive, as if I'm a little girl and what I'm upset about is silly and unimportant.

Self counselor: And when you heard those words, what happened inside?

Blimi: It makes me feel diminished, stupid, self-deprecating. That I must be an awful person to be so upset over nothing. And I feel misunderstood by him.

Self counselor: It must feel horrible to think your own husband, the most important person in your life, doesn't understand you.

Blimi: Exactly! Sometimes I wonder about our relationship, if we lack even that basic foundation.

Self counselor: I'm so glad you can admit your thoughts and feelings right now. I'm wondering if this is how you generally see him.

Blimi: I don't think so, but when he minimizes my pain, he seems harsh.

Self counselor: What might it remind you of from your past?

Blimi: My father always made light of anything I was upset about.

His mouth would twitch as if to stop a smile or laugh, and he'd say, "What are you so upset about, *mamala*, this is small potatoes. Nothing should bother you like this. Don't cry. Forget about it." He was always wanting me to be logical and less emotional. But I was just a little girl.

Self counselor: And?

Blimi: That made me think about what was bothering me even more, *and* I felt angry at myself because Tatty told me it was no big deal. So clearly there was something wrong with me. And I felt hurt on two levels, with no one to talk to about it. Because Mommy would support Tatty to be sure I didn't see him in a bad light.

Self counselor: Wow! You must have felt confused and hurt when looking for someone who could help you make sense of your feelings.

Blimi: I did! And, that's exactly how I feel now.

Self counselor: How did you get over it?

Blimi: Well, I guess I really didn't because that part of me easily flares when Zalmy says, "No big deal."

Self counselor: Hmmmm. Well, how (in any way) might you have drawn the "No big deal" response from Zalmy?

Blimi: [indignantly] I don't think I did. He always acts just like Tatty!

Self counselor: Always?

Blimi: Well, when he doesn't want me to feel bad.

Self counselor: Oh, why doesn't he want you to feel bad?

Blimi: [angrily] He hates to hear me complain and exaggerate.

Self counselor: [pauses and looks at her with compassion.]

Blimi: And, I guess if I think about it, he really feels awful when he thinks I'm in pain.

Self counselor: What tells you that?

Blimi: Well, if I allow myself to look at him at those times, I see sad eyes, as if he doesn't know what to do or say and just wants the discomfort to go away.

Self counselor: Uh-huh.

Blimi: I think it's difficult for him to see me upset.

Self counselor: Why is that?

Blimi: Because he really does care and wants the best for me.

Self counselor: How can you help him be there for you at those times?

Blimi: I could prepare him. Part of the problem is that he wants to jump in and fix it for me, not realizing that I just need him to listen. So, I might say, "Zalmy, could you please hear about my feeling upset for a minute so I can get it out of my system? I know in the long run it's no big deal, but at the moment it's giving me heartache, even worse than my mother's cinnamon apple kugel."

Self counselor: [Laughing] Worse than your mother's sickeningly sweet kugel? Oh my goodness. That's got to be the worst discomfort. I remember that kugel. Really lethal.

Blimi: [laughs]

Self counselor: What might happen if you asked him that?

Blimi: I think he would listen.

Self counselor: Wonderful. And what do you think Hashem wants?

Blimi: I think Hashem wants two things. He wants me to be more confident in my own skin, and he wants me to have more of a sense of humor about what others say. Not to take it so seriously… And he wants me to communicate my needs to my husband honestly, understanding the good intention behind my husband's behavior. He really is a good man, you know. When I'm not in this upset state, I recognize that.

Self counselor: In what ways is he really a good man?

Blimi: He works very hard for the family, he's sweet and loving most of the time, he gives a lot of time and attention to our children, he encourages me to take time for myself, to do the activities I enjoy, to take time with my friends, and he really wants to be there for me, no matter what. I just need to tell him more clearly how he could best support me.

Self counselor: Sounds like a wonderful plan.

Blimi: Thank you. I can breathe again. I think I'll go make a nice dessert for Zalmy. One that won't give him heartburn.

They both laugh.

■ ■ ■

Zalmy: Oy, I just don't know what to do with Blimi. She gets so rattled when someone says anything to her that she doesn't want to hear.

Self counselor: That sounds like a difficult situation for you.

Zalmy: It is! And then when I try to help, she attacks me with a laundry list of how I disappoint her.

Self counselor: That can't be much fun, to say the least.

Zalmy: Fun? Who can have any fun when their wife is so angry with them?

Self counselor: True, it colors everything in life and clearly impacts you deeply.

Zalmy: It sure does. It makes me feel like all my efforts to please her don't even register. They're worthless. I'm worthless. And I just want to get as far away as possible to avoid getting any more assaults on my character.

Self counselor: You want to escape from the pain and feeling of not getting it right with her. Do you recall ever feeling this way before?

Zalmy: My mother, whom I adored, would get so upset at the littlest things that others said, and it would make me feel powerless to help. I just couldn't please her no matter how I tried. I'd offer something, and she'd just get angrier at me, as if I got in the way of her need to let her feelings out about something else, and then I became the focus of her disturbance. It was very scary. I wanted to help, and I just added fuel to the fire.

Self counselor: So what did you do?

Zalmy: I'd run to my room and learn Gemara until I heard her puttering around in the kitchen and singing. That would be my signal that reentry was safe, and she was back to her normal, loving self.

Self counselor: That sounded like a good coping mechanism on your part. And you even used the time to study. What a smart thing to do. And now, knowing what you know about your wonderful wife and mother and their sensitivity to how others see them, what might you have done differently?

Zalmy: I have to remember that even though a friend's comment might seem silly, exaggerated, or unimportant in the long run from my perspective, to my sweet wife it could be devastating. I just don't want her to hurt. Especially over such nonsense. I think she's absolutely beautiful and always will be in my eyes.

Self counselor: What a wonderful thought about your wife. You are both so lucky to have each other. What might Hashem want from you at this time?

Zalmy: I think He would want me to step out of my past, to see that this is my dear wife who needs me and my mitzvah is to just listen compassionately for just a little bit. She never asks for a lot. She just needs me to be present and reflect her feelings. I don't have to be the big *macher* and fix everything. Listening tenderly is enough.

Self counselor: That sounds perfect! What a caring husband. Let me know how it goes.

PORCUPINE QUILLS

Malkie (pp. 61-66) works through her anger with her own inner-self counselor.

Malkie: I'm fuming. So glad Mom is leaving today. I just don't think I could take it anymore!

Self counselor: You sound very angry and upset.

Malkie: That's an understatement! Every time she comes, I go out of my way to be respectful and make her comfortable, and yet all I get is a barrage of criticism about how I ruined her son's life and hers. I hate to say it, but I feel like I'm a victim of verbal and emotional abuse.

Self counselor: That sounds very painful. You wish she would value your efforts and see the happy family you have with her son. Instead, she just seems to get stuck in "if only" land.

Malkie: Exactly. Am I really so bad? [Heavy tears]

Self counselor: Absolutely not. She's really tough to please, and I feel for you.

Malkie: Really? I appreciate that.

Self counselor: Well, yeah. You said it yourself. Her words are abusive even if that isn't her intention. That's hard for anyone to deal with, don't you think?

Malkie: It has been very hard and frustrating. I want to love her and have a close connection, yet somehow I always end up feeling that I'm a disappointment to her…and that hurts. And then there's the value around money that seems to be at the root of a lot of the friction. We don't have the money for all the things I wish we could give the *kinderlach*, but I really don't care about fancy clothes and jewelry like she does. I mean, it certainly would be easier if Shalom had a more lucrative income. We have been blessed with a large family, and there are so many expenses. But he truly loves his work and is so good at it, and the students grow and value his guidance. And even more importantly, our children look up to their Tatty and love him dearly.

Self counselor: It sounds like you are generally happy with the way your family life is going but your mother-in-law touches a nerve, otherwise, why would this be so upsetting?

Malkie: I guess there is a part of me that resents the struggle and wishes we didn't have to count our pennies so carefully. Most of the time I'm happy, yet somehow, when she speaks about finances, it brings up my own feelings of worry and uncertainty. Somehow, I want to prove to her that true wealth lies in a Torah life and I wish she would see it when she looks at us. When she appears to find fault, I feel inadequate, as if I'm not doing a good enough job demonstrating the beauty of Torah life. If she equates our lifestyle with deprivation on my account, I've failed miserably.

Self counselor: That's a lot. It sounds like part of you wishes you could have more money and the other part is very grateful for the gifts you have and the choices you have made. And you feel this strong pressure to prove to your mother-in-law that you're all thriving. What's the worst part for you, assuming that all of these feelings are grounded in truth?

Malkie: I feel shame that we may not have enough to take care of them or we'll have to sacrifice our family's needs to provide for them as they begin to age. I also feel guilty that I find it hard to love my mother-in-law unconditionally. She's such a thorn in my self-esteem.

Self counselor: It's a tough one. Hard to love someone who's so critical, especially in an area where you feel so vulnerable.

Malkie: But she's still my husband's mother. Her blood is carried in my children. And it's normal for her to fear aging and becoming dependent. Who can she count on if not us?

Self counselor: That's very generous and compassionate of you, dear Malkie.

Malkie: Thank you.

Self counselor: How can I help you feel more generous and compassionate toward yourself?

Malkie: Well, the affirmation you just gave me was a good start. I need to know that my mother-in-law's assessment of me isn't who I am, nor does it define me. I need to endorse myself for supporting Shalom in choosing his own path and pursuing his dreams.

Self counselor: Mmhmmm… and?

Malkie: I want to remind myself that underneath my mother-in-law's quills is a heart full of fear for the well-being of her family and trepidations for her own future. So I have to stop allowing it to trigger me and send me into a frenzy of self-recrimination. It's really hers and not mine. And, I'm not going to change her. The only one I have any control over is myself.

Self counselor: That's pretty impressive work you just did. It truly is. I'm so honored to be a part of your journey of self-acceptance and realization.

Malkie: Thank you. I can breathe again. Believe it or not, there is even a small voice, a whisper, that wants her to come again before too long, so I can try not to be triggered in the same way after coming to this realization.

Self counselor: Wow! Malkie, I really respect the person you are and who you are striving to be.

FIRED!

Zahava (pp. 111-116) utilizes the ICARE Model after being fired, working as her own inner-self counselor.

Zahava: I can't believe my boss fired me. Me? After all I've done for them? Are they kidding? I thought I was getting a raise, and now this?! I just can't reconcile this. How could she?! This is so totally devastating!

Self counselor: Sounds awful...

Zahava: It *is* awful. What am I missing? Did I do something wrong? I revamped their systems, made everything run more smoothly and efficiently; is this how they repay good work? I'm just so terribly upset.

Self counselor: Makes perfect sense that this would be upsetting. Who wouldn't be after all that effort? What's the worst part?

Zahava: It makes me doubt myself. As much as I'm upset with them, I wonder if I did something wrong. So I blame myself, and my self-esteem, which was pretty high while I was working, just took a nosedive. I feel so unappreciated, and at the same time I question my worth.

Self counselor: I'm so sorry. Sounds very sad and hurtful. What might this remind you of from your past?

Zahava: I hadn't even thought of the past, but now that you mention it, it reminds me of a time when I was twelve and the choir leader chose my friend for a solo instead of me. I really thought I had better pitch and more expression. Her decision shocked me just like now. And the same words, "It's not fair!" want to scream out of my throat. It truly feels just as unfair as when I was a young child.

Self counselor: Very interesting! How are these two situations similar?

Zahava: Well, the similarities are quite strong because in both situations I did a job that I really believed was worthy of commendation. But, instead of being valued, they let me go; I was dispensable. What person would want to feel like a paper towel tossed out once it's fulfilled its purpose?

Self counselor: [shaking her head back and forth in commiseration and silently asking me to continue]

Zahava: Being rejected hurts so badly, especially when I truly feel qualified and capable. It would still hurt if that weren't the case, but at least on some level, it would make sense. And the idea of telling my husband that I no longer have a job seems so humiliating. It sets off my anger all over again when I think about the ramifications of this loss. Couldn't they have creatively designed a way to keep me onboard if they truly valued what I brought to the table?

Self counselor: It's not just the fact that they laid you off, but the implications of it as well?

Zahava: Exactly! Adjustment to a new reality takes time, as it definitely came as a shock. And it makes me see how much my identity is tied up with my employment status. Ugh. Do I need other people to tell me that I have talents to feel good about myself? So hard to realize that there is still part of me that craves the gold stars.

Self counselor: It takes a lot of courage and honesty to look at yourself so openly. Very impressive!

Zahava: Thank you. I guess I need to stay with these thoughts and feelings for a little while and try to understand why this is so significant for me.

Self counselor: Yes! If you let yourself feel your feelings and think about the current situation and how it ties back to other events in your life, you'll be able to understand and come to terms with it.

Zahava: Right, because if I give myself permission to feel my feelings and then think about it from the perspective of the bigger picture, I'll be able to move beyond in a healthier way. I want to learn from this experience. And you know, when one door closes, another opens. I trust that everything that occurs is designed to help me grow and will ultimately be for my benefit even if it is hard to perceive in the moment.

Self counselor: Excellent! You're already doing this work right here and now! It must feel deeply satisfying.

Zahava: It really does. I want to get back on track, moving toward my ideal self.

Self counselor: Your ideal self? Who is she? How is she different from the self that is here and now?

Zahava: She's more logical, reasonable, calm, and able to handle challenges without losing her sense of self-respect.

Self counselor: How can we encourage that part of yourself?

Zahava: I can open myself up and be vulnerable, which will invite warmth and encouragement from my loving family and friends. They really are very supportive and will not judge me as I do.

Self counselor: Excellent! Wow. I can tell from your calmer demeanor and slower heart rate that you're already beginning to feel better. I'm so happy for you and proud of you, my dear little self.

Zahava: [blushing shyly] Thank you.

Self counselor: [beams an illuminated smile at me, encouraging me to continue.]

Zahava: [Animated] And, in addition, I can take my boss up on writing a sincere letter of recommendation.

Self counselor: [nods in agreement.]

Zahava: And you know what? I really need to remind myself that any particular job doesn't define my identity. I'm the same person today as I was yesterday while sitting at that desk, except perhaps more sensitive and compassionate toward people who may have gone through similar challenges.

Self counselor: Excellent!

Zahava: I'm reflecting on how I can grow from this challenge. It's so interesting that in acknowledging my hurt feelings instead of pretending they don't exist, in thinking it through with you, the pain subsides and I find myself experiencing more self-acceptance and a place of inner serenity.

Self counselor: That's heartwarming and incredibly insightful.

PASSING THE BUCK

Basya (pp. 124-131) uses the ICARE model to work through her hurt at being criticized for misallocating *tzedakah* funds.

Self counselor: You seem upset, what's going on?

Basya: I tried to do something good and instead I got yelled at.

Self counselor: That must hurt.

Basya: It really did and made me angry. It felt unjust.

Self counselor: So what happened? What did she do that was so upsetting?

Basya: She accused me of not following the protocol and trying to be pushy about how the money should be allocated.

Self counselor: And...

Basya: I didn't know that I couldn't earmark funds. I had no idea that I was stepping on her toes. I just wanted to help Shiri. That poor lady is really struggling and here it is right before Pesach. Her pain was intense. I couldn't just sit there and not do something for her. I knew there was something I could do. My intentions were pure.

Self counselor: So what did Raizy do that was so upsetting?

Basya: She made it sound like I was purposely going around her, like I was sneaking. I almost felt like a naughty child getting caught red-handed.

Self counselor: Uh huh, it sounds like you feel a need to defend yourself.

Basya: That's exactly right. She was condescending. Like I should have known, like it was so blatantly clear — but it wasn't. I had done similar fundraising with the Rabbi's fund and it was perfectly accepted and actually appreciated. I just wanted to help. And I thought of Raizy as someone I respected and who was such a kind person. I thought she would be delighted. Instead, she felt put upon and overlooked. Ugh. Exactly the opposite of what I expected to happen.

Self counselor: What might this remind you of from the past?

Basya: I'm thinking... When something I thought was for the good, backfired... Hmmmmm. What comes to mind is doing my sister's chores and getting in trouble with my mother, because Mommy wanted her to do her own chores.

Self counselor: Good! Tell me more. What did that feel like?

Basya: I knew my sister hated to clean and I really enjoyed it. So when I told her I'd take care of her work so she could go spend time with her friends, I thought I was doing a mitzvah. Instead, my mother got angry at me and my sister. I felt sad, disappointed, and confused, wondering how a good deed could backfire like that. And even guilty that I got my sister in trouble when I was just trying to help.

Self counselor: How did your mother express her upset?

Basya: It wasn't only what she said but the way she said it. Made me feel guilty, like I was doing something sneaky and underhanded rather than praising me for my extra work that would allow my sister to have joy. Shouldn't I have gotten a little praise for my selflessness?

Self counselor: It was very kind of you to want to help your sister enjoy herself and your mother's response must have been painful. Do you think, perhaps, your mother was trying to protect you and your sister at the same time?

Basya: Well, it didn't feel like it at the time, but I do tend to overextend myself and then get exhausted or cranky and can feel underappreciated for all I do.

Self counselor: That makes sense.

Basya: I understand in retrospect that perhaps I should have found out about the guidelines around distributing *tzedakah*. I thought what I was doing was fair and just, but I can see that even though I found the money for Shiri, perhaps it wasn't my place to tell the agency how to distribute it. I didn't know. I just didn't know.

Self counselor: Wow. That acknowledgment took a lot of courage, self-reflection, and honesty. I don't know how many people could be that honest with themselves.

Basya: Thank you. [Deep breath] It's not easy to take a close look at yourself when you're enveloped in a mitzvah halo. Somehow that makes everything seem kosher.

Self counselor: That's the hardest time to try to grow, when you feel you've done something out of all good intentions. Makes total sense to me that you would feel unappreciated and misunderstood under the circumstances.

Basya: I need to breathe and realize that in the crisis of someone's need, perhaps I could pause and reflect on possibilities. Maybe if I had, I'd have taken the money to the Rabbi's fund instead. Or I could have found out more about how this fund works instead of forging ahead, like a knight in shining armor. When I think about it now, it would make sense that Raizy could have felt insulted or belittled by my trying to be the savior while she was adhering to the rules. Maybe I hurt her feelings while I was being self-righteous about my actions.

Self counselor: You are amazing! What an incredible insight. Look how far you've journeyed from your initial reactions of anger and hurt to having compassion for Raizy. That's truly extraordinary. I'm in awe.

Basya: [Blushes and murmurs] Thank you. I loved my sister so much and she hated housework. She was much more extroverted and blossomed in her interactions with others. And she always made a difference with them. But I'm a homebody and I love doing things that make our home a little nicer. I just didn't understand why Mommy wanted us to do the same work. It was so satisfying to me to see my sister happy, so why couldn't I do more of the housework while she made us look good in the community? It seemed like a fair trade to me. Especially when she came home glowing and I could benefit from her light spirit. And I emulated her and wanted to be more like her. When I reached out to the benefactors, I felt like my sister's wonderful way of contacting people and inviting their collaboration was inside of me. I learned that from her. It was a blessing.

Self counselor: And nothing that happened here takes any of that away from you.

Basya: That's true but if I truly want to do this mitzvah in a complete way, I think I'll go apologize to Raizy. I'd much rather do a mitzvah without any rough edges.

Self counselor: That sounds like a wonderful idea for a growing person like you.

A TELLING MOMENT

Kayla (pp. 142-148) successfully works through her fear of sharing her illness with Shalom using the ICARE model.

Kayla: I'm so frightened that Shalom is going to reject me for my health issues.

Self counselor: It is scary to reveal yourself and be vulnerable when you like him and see him as a possible life partner.

Kayla: It really is! How will I feel if he no longer wants me? And if he walks away, will any possible *shidduch* work out? Will I ever be able to get married? [Tears forming]

Self counselor: [softly] You really are terrifying yourself about this, aren't you?

Kayla: Well, how else can I feel? It really is terrifying. I don't want to tell him. And what could be more important than finding the right marriage partner? And [voice trembling as fear mounts again] if I don't reveal the truth, what kind of partnership would that be? I can't live a lie.

Self counselor: That's for sure. You want a relationship built on trust. Do you think that there is more going on inside of you than meets the eye? What might this remind you of from your past? When else have you been frightened like this about the possibility of being rejected?

Kayla: That's just it. Never. I lived a charmed life. I was loved by my friends, cherished by my family. I excelled in school and was respected by my teachers. It was almost as if I had the magic touch. Everything was so easy and so rewarding. Until that awful diagnosis.

Self counselor: Awful?

Kayla: Yes. Now I might not be good enough. I'm no longer the perfect-wife candidate. I'm damaged goods now.

Self counselor: Maybe it's a blessing in disguise.

Kayla: What do you mean? How could this be any kind of blessing?

Self counselor: Well, what do you think?

Kayla: Well…you may be right. It's teaching me humility and not to take my blessings for granted. I appreciate my health more than I ever did. I have more compassion for others when they're struggling. I think I might not have been so accepting before. I think it will probably make me a better mother, able to empathize with my babies when they're unhappy.

Self counselor: And that's a damaged person?

Kayla: Well, maybe not so bad.

Self counselor: So even if this particular *shidduch* isn't the right one, someone with such caring traits and other stellar qualities has to be a wonderful prospect for the right man.

Kayla: Do you think the right man will see me beyond my illness?

Self counselor: You are far more than this problem that you're suffering and it doesn't define you. It's just a condition that comes and goes. I believe you will resolve it for the best.

Kayla: Thank you for believing in me! I'm going to face my fear and I'll tell Shalom, and, with Hashem's support, I know it will be all right, whatever the result.

CONCLUSION

Dear Readers,

We hope you have enjoyed relating to the characters in this book as much as we did. The more we put ourselves in their shoes, the closer and more compassionate we felt toward them. As we observe, we learn. As our defenses go down when we look at others, our openness to self-awareness is heightened. Allow us to respond to a couple of frequently asked questions.

1. **When do I work on solving these issues with my own self as therapist, and when do I seek professional help?**

    If the issue continues to torment you and interfere with your quality of life and your attention to your family and responsibilities, it is time to seek professional assistance. Asking for help demonstrates courage and a deep desire to grow. Sometimes, we all need an objective listener to help us uncover the obstacles that prevent us from moving forward.

If there is any danger of abuse or emotional manipulation, please seek help immediately.

2. I thought negative emotions like anger and jealousy are wrong. Why should I acknowledge them?

The way to rid ourselves of negative emotions that we experience isn't by pretending they don't exist. In that case, they will fester and erupt or hurt us in other ways. If we truly want to rid ourselves of unwanted anger, for example, then only by being genuine and owning when we notice our anger and what triggers it, can we hope to diminish it, except in situations where it is appropriate.

3. Were we looking through your window when we wrote our book?

This is probably the most common reaction demonstrating the normalcy of human emotional responses and the *avodah* that we all share in terms of working on our *middos*.

The answer is no.

May Hashem help you actualize your potential and derive tremendous pleasure from all of your relationships.

Esther Gendelman, MS, LPC, CPC, and Rachel Stein

ABOUT THE AUTHORS

Esther Gendelman, MS, LPC, CPC, is a licensed psychotherapist and certified professional coach who specializes in working with relationships. She cherishes her own roles as wife, mother, and grandmother. A veteran educator, speaker, and shadchan, she has a passion for helping people grow and maximize their potential. She can be contacted at 248-915-9122 or at awindowwithin@gmail.com for speaking engagements, consultations, or counseling appointments in person or remotely. She welcomes your visits to her website at awindowwithin.net.

Living in the warm community of Atlanta, **Rachel Stein** keeps busy with her beautiful *berachos* as a wife, mother, and grandmother. In her spare time, she enjoys freelance writing and has authored a number of books for children and adults, including *Special Delivery* 1 and 2, *Growing with the Tree, The Story That Never Ends, Guilt-Free Chocolate, One Step at a Time, A Whale of a Time, The Royal Mission, Life Support,* and the soon-to-be-released *Whirl and Twirl.* It is also her privilege to be the copresident of Bikur Cholim of Atlanta.